THE COMPLETE BOOK OF
CAT BREEDING

Dan Rice, D.V.M.

BARRON'S

About the Author

Dan Rice is a retired small-animal veterinarian who is now pursuing his lifelong writing ambition. Although calico cats occupy a special place in his heart, he and his bride Marilyn have experienced ownership by various other types and breeds of cats throughout their more than 40 years of marriage.

Other Barron's titles by Dan Rice:
Bengal Cats: A Complete Pet Owner's Manual (1995)
The Complete Book of Dog Breeding (1996)

All inquiries should be addressed to:
Barron's Educational Series, Inc.
250 Wireless Boulevard
Hauppauge, New York 11788

International Standard Book No. 0-8120-9764-5

Library of Congress Catalog Card No. 96-21778

Library of Congress Cataloging-in-Publication Data
Rice, Dan, 1933–
   The complete book of cat breeding / Dan Rice.
      p.   cm.
   Includes bibliographical references (p.) and index.
   ISBN 0-8120-9764-5
   1. Cats—Breeding. I. Title.
SF449.5.R48   1996
636.8′082—dc20   96-21778
                                                  CIP

Printed in China

9876543

Acknowledgments and Dedication

The great pleasure experienced in writing this book was in large part due to the encouragement, assistance, and support of Barron's editor Mary Falcon. The quality of this volume, like one of my previous books, has also been enhanced by the knowledgeable evaluation and critique of Fredric Frye, D.V.M., M.S. A note of thanks is also due to a local veterinarian and friend, Steve Wanick, D.V.M., for providing unlimited access to his professional library.

Throughout the months spent researching and writing this book, I have been encouraged by a friend of nearly 13 years. She has spent much of each working day curled up on my lap, rubbing her chin on my keyboard, and nibbling at my wrist when I neglect her. Though my work has been slowed some by her need for attention, the pleasure of writing has been heightened by Sally, to whom I dedicate this book.

Cover Photos

Front cover: Balinese mother and kittens; inside front cover: ten-week old silver tabby Persian; inside back cover: adult male Devon rex; back cover: American curl kittens.

Photo Credits

Chanan: pages 13, 26, 48, 56, 76, 78; Donna Coss: pages 90, 137; Susan Green: pages 24, 30, 51; Leslie Hall: page 131; Don Himsel: pages 6, 29, 104, 105, 112; Jane Howard: pages 23, 87; Larry Johnson: page 136; Walter Magli: page 113; Mark McCullough: inside front cover, inside back cover, back cover; pages 3, 4 top and bottom, 5, 9 top, 16, 17, 19, 20, 33, 37, 43, 61, 64, 72, 117, 122, 126, 142; Terri Pattison: pages 94, 127; Marilyn Rice: page 41; Bob Schwartz: front cover; pages 9 bottom, 12, 49, 58, 59, 60, 67, 79, 80, 81, 82, 93, 99, 103, 107, 109, 116, 120, 129, 133, 135, 140; Gulliver Spring: page 144; Judith Strom: page 10.

Important Note

Always use caution and common sense whenever handling a cat, especially one that may be ill or injured. Employ proper restraint devices as necessary. In addition, if the information and procedures contained in this book differ in any way from your veterinarian's recommendations concerning your pet's health care, please consult him/her prior to their implementation. Finally, because each individual pet is unique, always consult your veterinarian before administering any type of treatment or medication to your pet.

Contents

Chapter 1

Introduction

About this Book

Our fascination with the species *Felis catus* is natural, considering that felines are among the most interesting and intelligent animals on earth. Human enchantment with cats predates history. Pictographs on cave walls and inside Egyptian tombs offer proof of the important roles of cats in ancient human cultures. Each time a domestic house cat strolls across the living room floor, its carriage and bearing mimic the regal power and splendor of its larger cousins. Great cats, including the enormous Asian tigers, African lions, and American pumas, have long been held in awe. Like those larger models of the Felidae family, the house cat hasn't yielded to subjugation by humans.

Cat breeding is an ancient craft, one that has been studied and practiced for centuries. Although this book concentrates on cat reproduction, many appealing side trips will provide insight into the species—its habits, origin, and place in history.

With its primary purpose to accumulate, record, and add to available knowledge about feline reproduction, this book addresses all cat breeders, who comprise three general categories.

- **Professional cat breeders** enter a cat breeding endeavor seriously, with carefully planned agendas and well-defined motives. You attended cat shows, selected a fascinating breed, learned all you could about the breed, and eventually purchased your breeding stock. Even if that stock is a singular, eight-week-old kitten, you are a budding professional cat breeder.

  This book will help you every step of the way. Brood animal selection and care, nutrition, breeding, pregnancy, queening (giving birth), and many other subjects are covered in depth, and include information not easily accessible from other breeders or breed specialty books. A lifetime of experience is combined herein, with facts and data from the latest veterinary literature.

- **Novice cat breeders** may have obtained a purebred cat as a pet. As its personality and character matured, you were stimulated to study the breed and enter your pet in a show or two. To your delight it was a winner! As its superior quality was identified, and after carefully examining the kitten market, you are now thinking about breeding the animal. You might be considered an incidental or novice cat breeder. You enjoy your pet and wish to share it with others. The pet and its health are your primary concerns, but you wish to produce a litter or two of the best kittens possible. You accept responsibility for your actions and need to know more about cat breeding.

This book is intended to familiarize you with the breeding process, dystocias (difficult births), dam and kitten feeding, detecting and solving breeding problems, raising kittens, vaccinations, examinations, and interviewing prospective buyers.

- **Accidental breeders** are responsible pet owners who acquired a cute kitten for the kids. It's a nice pet, but of questionable ancestry and not of exhibition quality. Because some folks consider it natural for cats to spend much of their lives wandering the neighborhood, you may have allowed it to go outside every night. Then one day when it was about six months old, your cat began to gain weight. Suspicions aroused, a quick trip to a veterinarian confirmed that she is about to have kittens; however it is too late to correct the problem. What you need now is good advice that will help you cope with your anguish and make the best of the situation. By offering options and giving instructions and advice, this book will help you emerge from an undesirable position with a healthy dam and kittens.

This is a generic book; one that fits all cat reproduction situations. Pregnancy determination as well as termination—spaying and castration, when, how, and why—are discussed. Much of the text refers to specific cat breeds and the purposeful mating of selected animals. Lest you misunderstand, please note that the wonderful mixed-ancestry felines found on doorsteps or in shopping baskets in front of the supermarket are no different than purebreds regarding their value as pets and their care, health, and reproduction.

Cats as Pets

People select cats as family pets for a multitude of reasons. Most are pleased with their choices and only a few unfortunate owners, who didn't prepare themselves for cat relationships, are disappointed. If you happen to be one of those individuals who never owned a cat, you might be interested in some general information about *Felis catus.*

A word of warning: people often choose cats as pets for the wrong reasons. Are you seeking a pet that is easily dominated, devoted to and dependent on its owners? One that is easily trained and submissive at all times? Do you like animals but don't plan to spend much time with them? Do you want a nice small pet that requires practically no care, and doesn't shed; one that can go in and out at will and rarely bothers you? If so, I suggest you think twice about getting a cat!

Cats are individuals with dynamic personalities. They need responsible owners who will honor their individualities. They usually enjoy important places in their households, and often have you jumping through their hoops. The human world is made up of *ailurophiles* (those who love cats) and *ailurophobes* (people who fear, and consequentially hate, cats).

Isn't it interesting that people who love dogs often comment on the canine's loyalty, training, physical prowess, and capabilities? Guide dogs, pointers, retrievers, guard dogs, scent dogs, and sled dogs are all valued for what they can do for humans physically. Likewise, people who fear dogs are usually afraid of the animals from a purely physical standpoint. They know that trained guard dogs or vicious animals can inflict serious bodily damage.

Cats, on the other hand, are loved because of their emotional appeal. They do little for us physically, but bring quiet peaceful influences on our emotional lives. Their purring is universally recognized as the music of contentment, but no one knows exactly how the sound is made. Cats won't bring your slippers and newspapers, and rarely do tricks, but their idiosyncrasies and curious habits will entertain you.

Those who fear and hate cats can rarely explain their feelings of ani-

Exotic shorthair.

mosity. Certainly they aren't afraid of being physically attacked. Rather, they fear and hate cats because they don't understand them; they refuse to befriend and accept cats because cats carry their own credentials. Pet cats aren't carbon copies; all are originals.

All Felidae have anatomical, physiological features and behaviors that are unique, one of which is their propensity to shun conflict in their society. It is commonly called avoidance behavior, or behavior induced by adverse stimuli. There are three types of avoidance: *active* or fleeing from adversity: *passive* or freezing and standing motionless when trouble is perceived: and *protective* reflexes that include hiding. Most animals possess and display one or two of these behavioral traits. Cats have all three, and each is believed to be coordinated separately by specific regions of the brain.

All felines are powerfully built and athletic, yet they rarely display that

strength, using it sparingly to satisfy their own needs or desires. They are never seen actively chasing their prey, preferring to use their cleverness and cunning to catch it.

White Persian.

Whereas a dog may pursue a rabbit until both are exhausted, a cat employs patience, waiting motionless until the mouse is within the range of a quick feline jump and dispatching its quarry quickly with its sharp shearing teeth. A cat's tiny, compact feet that make delicate tracks on your countertop expand to double their usual size when their sharp retractile claws protrude to catch a rodent.

A cat's sense of smell is not as well developed as a dog's, but the feline's vision is better and its hearing is phenomenal. Its large eyes are accommodated to function well in low levels of light, and often incorrectly believed to be able to see in total darkness. The retinas of its eyes have a layer of guanine that produces an eerie reflection when light is shined toward them. A cat's acute sense of hearing is enhanced by ears that are equipped with about 30 separate muscles, allowing them to turn in every direction.

Cats possess great intelligence, but only accept special training by humans when it suits them. They are exasperatingly stubborn when you attempt to stop them from lying on their chosen sofa pillow, but they can learn to retrieve in minutes if you offer to play with them. I have known self-taught cats to knock at doors or jump up and ring a bell when they want to enter the house. Just try to train the same cat to perform those tricks for less of a reward than a warm hearth on a cold evening. The trained felines often seen on television and in movies respond to conditioning, and their trainers will usually confess that in the absence of the expected reward, their training wanes quickly. Cats will work, but only for tangible, acceptable wages!

People who try (and fail) to categorize cats usually don't like them. Folks who insist on being in command of every situation rarely appreciate feline roommates. Fortunately, the good guys are winning, and for many excellent reasons.

Cats come in colors to match practically any decor, with personalities to blend with almost everyone. Given the opportunity, most cats are affectionate and quiet. Others can be playful, clownlike creatures that bring laughter and happiness to entire families. At the same time, all cats possess inherent dignity not seen in any other pet species.

Cleanliness is another characteristic attributed to cats, and rightly so. How many other mammals have you seen spend hours washing and grooming themselves? Cats are able to reach nearly every square inch of their bodies with tongues that are covered with tiny papillae (projections), simulating hairbrushes. Even their skeletal structure accommodates complete cleaning. A cat's collarbone, or clavicle, is undeveloped and not connected with other skeletal structures, thereby allowing the head to pivot almost 180 degrees. These features enable cats to reach areas not accessible to other animals.

Pet felines are aloof and independent at times, yet they are covetous

rascals that can worm their ways into your heart, quietly bringing you into total servitude. Pet stores may suggest that all you need to own a cat is a litter box, food, and water. Don't believe it! Within a month after obtaining a furry little kitten, you will be seeking ways to please it. First, you buy a couple of small toys. Then, perhaps a soft, cuddly bed for it. A carpeted climbing perch with little sleeping compartments may follow; and of course three or four different types of scratching posts are needed.

Soon your home is properly furnished with feline furniture. At least one room in the house sports a covered, deodorized litter box with a swinging door. Stainless steel water and food bowls are positioned beside the refrigerator, and at least four flavors of expensive canned cat food occupy a special cupboard shelf. We obtain cats for our pleasure, but an insidious role reversal often takes place very early in the relationship.

Bluepoint Himalayan. The Himalayan breed was derived by combining the Persian and the Siamese.

Cat furniture.

ing dogs by 64 million to 53 million. There are many good reasons for their popularity. They are small, generally quiet, clean, and easy to live with, and, if kept indoors, they will often attain ripe old ages with minimal health care costs.

A variety of colors and personalities are strong selling points for cats. There is truly a cat breed for every taste. Dozens of recognized breeds share the generic and species name *Felis catus,* but habits and attitudes are quite dissimilar from breed to breed. Differences in appearance are startling in some cases, as you will confirm when you attend your first cat show. Long, thin bodied, svelte Siamese with sky blue eyes, big erect ears, and eerie voices hardly resemble the boxy, drop-eared Scottish Folds. Yet they are all *Felis catus.*

Bengal cats are stamped with the colors and coat patterns of their wild Asian jungle ancestors, yet they are docile, lovable pets. Aristocratic Persians with long beautiful coats and pug faces always seem to be posing for cameras. The squirrel-like colors and mischievous personalities of Abyssinians are intriguing. There is surely a breed for everyone, and every breed has certain characteristic traits peculiar to its members.

Even cats of the same breed display personalities and temperaments that vary between individuals. Like children, their manners and habits are malleable; their attitudes are partly learned—conditioned by their

I sometimes think that if cats had opposable thumbs, they would challenge us for superiority in our own world. But they will never mount that challenge because they already have the better of us at every turn of the wheel. Most homes are incomplete without a cat. Data now suggests that cat owners live longer and happier lives than those unfortunates who haven't yet discovered feline friendships. Cats are often maintained in nursing homes and other care facilities because residents are more at peace with the world when they have a cat to pet. I know of no better way to relax after a difficult day than sitting in my favorite chair, stroking our cat Sally, watching her feet kneading in time with her purring song.

Cats are now the number one house pets in America, outnumber-

human families. Those people who have shared their lives with cats of different breeds recognize that their pets' characters are deeper than the color and length of their coats.

Feline History

Long before professional cat breeding popularized the species as pets, cats were recognized as unique creatures and desirable companions. Historically, they have always occupied important places in human societies. Although cats were probably among the last wild animal species domesticated by humans, they have been prominent in human cultures throughout the ages.

Since domestication, dogs have been molded into hundreds of sizes and shapes. Their anatomy and personalities have been altered to serve dozens of different purposes, ranging from fighting each other to catching rats; from pulling sleds to retrieving ducks. Ancient history reveals some domestic dogs' ancestors resembling large, bulky wolves; others were small, more streamlined, somewhat similar to sight hounds. Cats, however, remain about the same size and shape of their wild progenitors.

If you accept evolutionary thinking, you might be interested to know that cats have been placed in the Pliocene epoch, about 7 million years ago. Unlike horses and dogs, who have theoretically evolved from very different appearing predecessors, cat creatures of that period are

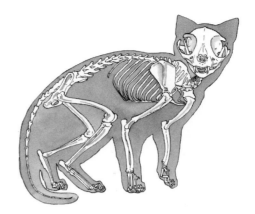

Feline skeletal structure.

said to be virtually identical to the domestic cats of today. Egyptian pictographic history of 3,500 years ago indicates the presence of cats that are believed by some to have been domesticated at that time. They were present in Crete as early as 1600 B.C., being portrayed in drawings as hunting cats. Histories of Greece place them in that part of the world in 500 B.C., and in India in 100 B.C., where they are recorded in Sanskrit documents. By A.D. 600 they appeared in the Middle East

Feline muscular structure.

Feline internal organs.

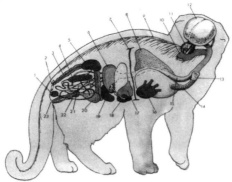

1. Testicles
2. Anus
3. Large intestine
4. Pancreas
5. Kidney
6. Stomach
7. Diaphragm
8. Lung
9. Spinal cord
10. Sinus cavities
11. Mouth cavity
12. Brain
13. Larynx
14. Trachea
15. Esophagus
16. Heart
17. Liver
18. Gall bladder
19. Spleen
20. Bladder
21. Small intestine
22. Spermatic cord
23. Penis

and in Japan, and were present in Great Britain in A.D. 936. Best guesses by experts place domestic house cats in the United States in 1750; however, a petroglyph from

ORDER: Carnivora
FAMILY: Felidae
GENUS: *Acinonyx* (cheetah)
Panthera (lion, tiger, leopard)
Felis (house cat, leopard cat, golden cat, ocelot, margay, lynx, caracal, mountain lion, jaguarundi, pampas cat, Andean cat, Palla's cat, clouded leopard, marbled cat, serval, fishing cat, flat-headed cat)

New Mexico may indicate that domestic appearing cats were known in Indian cultures in North America 3,000 years ago.

Paintings and carvings in Egyptian tombs show spotted felines of about the same size and conformation as our domestic tabbies. Humans have had little success changing the splendid physical appearance or the intangible personality qualities of felines. Cats are less genetically plastic than dogs and other mammals. There seems little reason for them to change because they seem to have achieved great success in their present form.

Classification of Cats

House cats share the genus *Felis* with many wild species. Their species name has been changed several times in technical literature. Once known as *Felis familiaris,* the accepted house cat taxonomic name is now *Felis catus.*

Felis subspecies do not typically live and hunt in packs or prides as do some other genera of the family Felidae. Their intelligence, agility, and athletic ability allow them to survive and thrive without dependence upon others of their species. Dogs and many other animals were dominated by humans and brought into submission and domestication by leadership and, later, trust. Cats are not great followers however, and probably decided to join in human fellowship to take advantage of feeding opportunities.

Their symbiotic roles in human civilizations no doubt stemmed from their hunting prowess. It's likely that wild *Felis* species moved close to human society to feed on rodents that were attracted to granaries, pantries, and food preparation areas. Early Egypt was dependent upon grain production, which adds to the probability of feline domestication originating in that region. Later, perhaps feral cats entered human dwellings to scavenge bits of meat left by fireplaces, and there found warm cozy corners in which to make their nests. Their value in controlling food pests must have been easily recognized, and their cleanliness and independence were appreciated. I believe they were domesticated only by mutual consent after recognizing the advantages of human companionship.

Cats were courted and favored by humans centuries before they took the pet spotlight. When Egypt was the center of the world and pharaohs were worshipped by their subjects, cats shared the prominence of ruling families. Thousands of carefully preserved mummified cat bodies, which have been excavated from the tombs of pharaohs, give evidence of their importance in that ancient but literate society. The Egyptian goddess of light and music was depicted as a cat-headed figure who was benefactor of all cats. Cat protection laws were enforced and violators faced a death penalty if they were found responsible for killing a cat. Those Egyptians really

knew how to take care of their feline companions!

During the European Middle and Dark Ages, cats were feared and hated by the unlettered populations. Sorcerers, witches, practitioners of black magic, and devil worshipers

Top: Ruddy Abyssinian.

Bottom: The Somali, which is basically a longhaired Abyssinian.

Bengal kitten.

made use of cats. To see a black cat was an evil omen that would surely bring bad luck. Stories of those times relate ceremonies in which cats were tortured and executed by uneducated Christians who feared them as sinister spirits of Satan. They were believed to be supernat-

Animal shelters abound with stray and abandoned cats.

Name. *Jean*
Breed. *Bln ve 2 ½*
Reason *for surrender*

ural beings, possessing the souls of the devil and his companions.

The natural gifts of cats fed those fires of hate and fear. Cats walk and run noiselessly, high on their soft toe pads, moving quickly and silently through the night; they seemingly appear and disappear like phantoms, giving further evidence of their wickedness. Their vertebrae are held together by muscles and elastic tendons instead of the more rigid ligaments found in other domestic animals. That feature enables cats to elongate and contract their spines, oscillate, and bend their backs in curves. Being nocturnal hunters, they were perceived as shadows, specters, and creatures of darkness. Their contractile spines and clavicle structures add spring to their leaps, and their inherent athletic abilities allow them to jump to high places, vanishing like ghosts into treetops, over fences, or onto rooftops.

They possess vibrissae (tactile hairs) on their faces that allow them to measure the width of spaces before entering. Those long, thick, highly sensitive whiskers have individual sensory nerves leading to the brain. Cats slither noiselessly through narrow openings like magic, never getting stuck and never backing up. They are suspicious acting creatures that possess very little body odor and they secretively bury their excretions. Sleek, shiny, meticulously groomed, well-fed cats are commonly seen in communities populated by poorly fed, ragged, and tattered humans.

It is little wonder that cats were feared and hated by the uneducated masses. All that is past history. *Felis catus* is now firmly established as the country's favorite family pet. Unfortunately, that is not all good news.

Overpopulation

People sometimes obtain kittens as pets for their families, expecting their children to take responsibility for care of the pets. A questionable plan at best! Cute, helpless little kittens grow into independent adults that roam in and out of their homes unchaperoned. They are such adept survivors that most of them get along just fine when left to their own devices. They keep a low profile in the home until they reach sexual maturity. Then one day the family tomcat (intact male) comes home from a weekend adventure, exhibiting a torn ear or a swollen cheek. A few days later his wounds become

abscesses and begin to drain foul, purulent fluid. Or, if the pet is a *queen* (intact female), she returns from an overnight sojourn wearing a smile on her face, and in a few weeks her abdominal girth begins to expand.

Therein lies a major problem: Before any purposeful breeding discussion can be approached, one must consider the responsibility for pet stewardship.

Some people accept biblical accounts of Divine creation of the world's animals. Others prefer to believe that humans and their animals descended from a primordial ooze. In either case, there can be no doubt that humans share responsibility for managing the world's plants and animals. The plant and animal kingdoms preexisted people, and without them

Feral cats are a reservoir for the many contagious diseases that can threaten the health of house pets.

11

Outdoor cats are always at risk.

The Birman breed is thought to have originated in Burma.

people cannot survive. To allow any species to propagate without management is self-defeating.

Pet overpopulation figures are mind-boggling. It is painful to think of the millions of cats that are euthanized (humanely destroyed) in public animal shelters each year. That number is probably much lower than the number of homeless cats that die of disease and accidents. Additional millions of unwanted cats are

destroyed by owners or their veterinarians every year.

Feline overpopulation is not a parochial problem. It exists in heavily populated urban areas, suburbia, and the country. More studies are done in urban and suburban areas because homeless cats are more obvious in human-dense localities. The significance of overpopulation is many faceted.

Stray cats constitute a reservoir of infection for house cats. Respiratory infections are easily spread through window and door screens. Feline leukemia and other diseases are spread by contact between feral cats and house cats that have been allowed out into backyards. Outdoor cats are always at risk, both from infectious diseases and frequently fatal automobile accidents.

Homeless cats are innocent victims. The criminals are those thoughtless humans who allow their cats to breed indiscriminately and promiscuously and populate the world with ownerless, unwanted strays.

Reasons for Breeding

There are few legitimate reasons for breeding a queen. The reason I heard most frequently while in veterinary practice was the worst reason of all: "We want our children to learn all about the miracle of birth." Some people actually believed that a five-year-old child would absorb and retain significant information from watching a few kittens nurse. The likelihood of a child actually witnessing the birth process was remote. Fickle childhood concentration and interest might be initiated, but it is doubtful that any lesson would be learned and retained.

Parents who wish to teach their children about birth are well advised to purchase a couple of good books and video tapes that treat the subject objectively and effectively. Spare your neighbors and yourselves the trials of finding good homes for five or six nondescript kittens.

Only the best specimens should be allowed to enter any breed's gene pool. Before you purposefully breed a cat, you should assess the kitten market and accept steward-

ship for the animals produced under your control. To do otherwise is a disservice to yourself, your neighbors, and, most of all, to the beautiful cats of the world.

Another popular, but questionable reason for breeding cats is supplemental income: money! If you believe there is much money to be made by breeding fine quality purebred cats, I advise you to confer with several professional catteries that routinely show their cats. High prices may be charged for a prime kitten now and then, but when compared to the expenses inherent in good breeding management, there is precious little profit.

The common denominator of both those reasons for breeding a queen is lack of understanding of a breeder's responsibilities. Those obligations aren't met by displaying a basketful of kittens in a shopping cart in a parking lot. You are an equally poor steward when you donate a litter to a pet shop. Breeders of any animals, whether purebred or mixed, have the responsibility to locate homes for every kitten produced. That means identifying families who truly want your kittens and will provide lifelong safety, health care, food, housing, and love. Prospective owners should be carefully screened to prevent promiscuous breeding, and to minimize accident risks and other abuses.

In final analysis, there is one really good reason to purposefully breed a purebred queen: if she is an outstanding specimen and has proven her merit in the show ring—a queen that, when bred to an equally admirable tom, may produce kittens that are credits to the breed.

Cat breeding is a wonderful pastime. Properly managed, the hobby might even break even or cost you very little to pursue. You will find great satisfaction in producing excellent quality kittens, and watching your cats win ribbons in shows.

Other books about your specific breed will teach you the fine points of breed standard interpretation. Cat shows are practical exhibitions of breed standards. This book is designed to help you manage a cat breeding program from selection of brood animals to placing kittens into caring, loving homes.

Chapter 2

Selecting and Conditioning Breeding Stock

Once you have decided to breed cats, perhaps the first question to answer is which sex you plan to obtain. There are some very good reasons why many small breeding programs do not maintain tomcats.

Large catteries usually keep their breeding toms in kennels, but most cat breeders want their cats to have free run of their homes. The undesirable, sexually related habits of intact toms often preclude keeping them as house pets unless the owners can accept their peculiarities. If breeding toms are maintained in homes with other cats, they can be very obtrusive and disruptive. Even when a tom is the only pet in a household, his foul-smelling urine which is often sprayed on curtains, doorways and furniture, will usually relegate him to a kennel.

As a general rule, it is far more pleasant and realistic for small cat breeding operations to maintain only queens and look to the larger catteries for stud cats.

When choosing purebred animals with which to begin a cat breeding program, three separate but inter-related quality issues must be considered.

- **Health and nutritional status.** Health and nutrition are of critical importance and are discussed at length throughout this book. Genetics are touched upon in later sections as related to the health, weaknesses, and anomalies of breeding animals.
- **Temperament or personality.** Dispositions and attitudes of

Tomcats typically spray-mark their territories, whether indoors or outside.

15

Two closely related breeds: Persian (left) and exotic shorthair (right).

breeding animals are of considerable interest, and those topics receive significant attention below. Desirable attitudes are both learned and genetically related.

- **Comparison to breed standards**. Breed standards are developed and fixed by careful selection of breeding stock. Within a breed, genetic manipulation is highly specialized, and is a study in itself. Each particular breed has its own genetic concerns.

Genetics of Cat Breeds

Every time I attend a cat show I discover another interesting breed of cats. Having certain preconceived ideas of what cats should look like, I am amazed by the varieties of colors and shapes of cats being exhibited. Each breed has been developed by careful selection of desirable features. Animals that best display those characteristics are chosen as propagation stock. The unique ears in Scottish folds or the coats of rexes are examples of recessive genetic characteristics or mutations. Perpetuation of those breeds requires specific genetic knowledge, and certain breeding rules must be followed to prevent undesirable faults from cropping up.

Producing the variety of beautiful color points, uniquely shaped heads, and eye color mandates intimate genetic knowledge of Siamese cats. That knowledge is only acquired by extensive study and experience, and is a discipline that has taken decades of practical research to develop.

Inbreeding and linebreeding are genetic manipulation techniques used to develop and hold physical characteristics in the various breeds. There are risks involved in those techniques and I recommend leaving them in the hands of experienced cat breeders who are knowledgeable in the genetics of their breeds.

Information on the various intricacies of feline genetics would fill a library shelf. Scientific and backyard studies as well as controlled breeding experiments have been conducted for many years to establish color patterns, coat lengths, body conformation, eye colors, and various other peculiarities of the many breeds.

I have nurtured a fascination with calico cats for many years. Calico is not a breed, but a particular color combination: spotted or blotched white, red, and black colors in various shades and diverse patterns. Calicos are found in several breeds, but they share a unique genetic feature. Virtually all calico cats are females. That is, the odds of ever finding a calico male are about equal to buying a winning ticket in the lottery. I had the dubious honor of owning the only male calico I ever met. He was a domestic shorthair named Bob and he was given to me when he was six months old.

Bob was an interesting study. He was totally deaf and lacked normal balance. His equilibrium was nearly nonexistent; his gyro had a loose wire. He refused to jump onto or from anything taller than himself. When he attempted to jump down from a chair or footstool, he usually landed on his chin. He panicked when someone picked him up, and would cling with the claws of all four feet to prevent being dropped.

He was never litterbox trained and even showed disdain for outdoor sand piles. Feces and urine were deposited on the lawn, floor,

American shorthair.

sidewalk, or driveway at his convenience. That strange cat was a social outcast! Our other cats hated him and refused to associate with him under any circumstances. At first, I believed he was shunned because he was the only intact tomcat in our household, but it probably also related to his deafness and singular habits.

Bob was purposefully mated between 18 and 24 months of age to three different queens: two calicos and an orange tabby. All three queens exhibited obvious, receptive signs of estrus, and all had successfully raised kittens in the past. Bob was an eager, aggressive breeder, displaying all the typical moves of a proven stud, but his conception rate from those breedings was zero. (Dr. Fredric Frye of Davis, California and his colleagues have studied the chromosomal makeup of a number

Strong fiberglass carriers make traveling with your cats easier.

let habits didn't improve thereafter, and the other cats of the household continued to refuse to share their food or water. They virtually guarded the feeders from him. Fortunately, an attorney friend admired him and offered him a new home. He was a curious individual, but his story has little to do with cat breeding. I include this calico cat story only to illustrate an interesting feline genetic phenomenon.

of calico toms and have published technical papers on the subject. Their studies indicate, among other things, that all of the few extant calico males are infertile.)

Bob was an odd, interesting cat, but a poor pet. Eventually, I offered him to the university veterinary college for genetic studies, but they declined. I castrated him, but his toi-

Selecting a Queen and Having Her Examined

Before embarking on a cat breeding program, you will have attended cat shows, become fascinated with a particular breed, read books on that breed, and studied the breed standard. There are many fine specimens from which to make your selection, and you will need to find the right breeding animal, without regard to the particular breed or age.

I advise you not to consider taking a new kitten into your home before it is eight to ten weeks old. It should be energetically independent, eating well, and the picture of good health. Watch it closely in the breeder's home. Be sure it is curious, outgoing, and easily handled. Its age is secondary to its health and temperament. Be cautious about selecting a kitten that is shy and unfriendly. It probably isn't mature enough to leave the nest.

A veterinary examination should precede the final purchase of a new queen.

When a queen is selected, whether a just weaned kitten or an adult several years old, she should be thoroughly examined by a veterinary practitioner. It is wise to have the physical exam performed before her purchase is finalized, with guaranteed return privileges. In addition to the physical examination, the veterinarian will require a fecal sample to check her for intestinal parasites. In confined house pets, worms are easily controlled, but they are of great significance in any breeding program and must not be overlooked. A record of her vaccinations, diet, previous health checkups, blood tests, and fecal examinations should accompany her to the veterinary clinic.

In a well-managed breeding program, that initial examination may have been done before the kittens were advertised. If it was performed within the past week or two, and if complete records of the results of the examination are available, another exam may not be necessary. I recommend that you reserve the option of conferring with the examining veterinarian about the kitten before the purchase is finalized.

Many factors will be considered when that first examination is done. Her age, origin, condition, and health history dictate the extent of the examination. Your veterinarian may advise you of specific tests that are appropriate, such as blood examinations for the *Hemobartonella* organism, laboratory tests for feline leukemia virus, and others. Some

Tonkinese kittens.

diseases are endemic in one part of the country and virtually unknown in other areas.

If purchased as an adult, the queen's previous breeding history is vitally important. The number of litters she raised, queening dates, birth dates, numbers of kittens in each litter, survival rate, and birth and weaning weights also provide important information.

Her general health can be evaluated by your veterinarian. She will be examined for physical problems that you might miss, such as eye, ear, heart, or lung abnormalities. Her teeth and gums will be examined as well as the joints of her legs. Skin and coat abnormalities that might be unapparent to you may indicate ectoparasites or nutritional or hormonal problems. Abdominal palpation of an adult queen's reproductive tract adds to the information gleaned from a professional examination.

Calico Japanese bobtails.

Young kittens and adults that have not been vaccinated for a year can receive needed immunizations at the time of examination. Need for nutritional supplementation may be discussed if minor deficiencies are discovered or suspected by the examining veterinarian.

Temperament

When she is on the examination table, being handled and palpated by your veterinarian, a partial assessment of your queen's general temperament will be made. Cats always fuss at strangers unless the meeting is of their own choosing, but if handling brings on exaggerated resistance, she may have disposition problems. Sometimes personalities can be conditioned and problems can be resolved if training is begun early in life.

A cat's temperament can't receive too much attention, especially when the animal is used in breeding programs. If I had to choose between a purebred queen with a minor conformational fault joined to a beautiful, predictable disposition, and a grouchy cat displaying perfect conformation, I'd take the good temperament every time.

Genetic predisposition to crabbiness is only part of the problem; temperament is not totally inherited. To some degree, orneriness is a product of conditioning. A nice kitten may grow up to be an ill-humored adult if it is mishandled when young. I think the most cantankerous cats I ever met were those that had been terrorized as kittens by young children. Little people rarely torment pets purposefully, but they need special instruction in pet handling.

Parents often give their children very real-appearing stuffed toys, then laugh at them when they carry those toys around by their tails. They are not corrected when they throw the stuffed kitten across the room or stomp on it. When children are only one or two years old, it is difficult for them to immediately recognize the difference between a stuffed kitten and the real thing. Unfortunately, they learn the difference at the expense of some bitten fingers or scratched arms, and cats don't readily forget unpleasant episodes in their lives. Trust is lost on both sides.

I have found that correcting the sour temperaments of adult cats is problematical. If their bad attitudes are learned, you have a good chance that careful conditioning will reverse the situation. If their perversity is inherited, you are probably out of luck. How do you tell the difference? The best advice I have to offer is: don't buy an adult breeding animal with a bad disposition. It is certain you don't want to produce kittens with similar attitudes.

If you wish to try to recondition a cat to establish trust, a great deal of patience is required. It may take weeks of regular ego stroking to win her over. Frequent sessions of petting and grooming, combined with lots of lap time and spontaneous special treats may lead to success.

When purchasing an adult breeding queen to double as a pet in a household with children, I suggest that you arrange a trial period of at least two weeks. During that time, the children should be gradually introduced to the cat under close observation. Most cats love kids; their acquaintances quickly develop into lifelong bonds of friendship, mutual trust, and love. If very young children or older cats are involved, the get acquainted period takes longer.

Introducing a New Cat

All cats, but especially kittens, are overwhelmed by unfamiliar surroundings. They will often crawl into

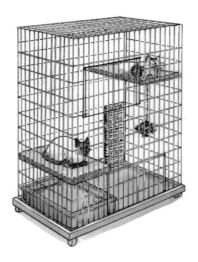

Confinement of the kitten is important for the first week in its new home.

some tiny space under a piece of furniture, or in the back of a closet, and remain there for a day or more. That is not a good way to begin your relationship with the cat.

Before taking the new cat home, ask the veterinarian to trim the prospective queen's claws. When introducing a kitten to children, snap judgments shouldn't be made when a child gets scratched. It may or may not be the cat's fault. Many times appropriate discipline is due to both the kitten and the child. Kittens will retaliate when hurt or frightened. Eight or nine week old kittens are resilient little creatures, but their tiny bones break easily when stepped on or dropped.

Confinement is important during the first few days a new kitten or adult cat is in your home. The newcomer can be maintained in a large kennel or in a small room, such as a bathroom, that is furnished with food, water, a blanket, and a litter

A wise cat breeder studies cat food labels carefully.

pan. Let it adapt to its new surroundings slowly, and minimize handling it for the first day or two. Then allow it to investigate its new home room by room for an hour or two before returning it to its room. After a week, it should be acquainted with the house and family and may be allowed to roam at will.

Nutrition

A good nutritional plan is the first consideration when designing a conditioning program. A well balanced diet in your queen will maximize the health of kittens produced and sustain the health of the parent. Once you have selected the best specimen of your chosen breed, had it examined, and treated any problems found, the next step in successful cat breeding is to establish a sound and effective feeding plan.

During many years of association with cats and their owners, I have learned that few people are inter-

ested in the technical data that usually accompanies a discussion of feline nutrition. Most cat owners want to get right to the bottom line, without wading through all the calculations. Because we rarely formulate our cats' diets in the kitchen, little is served by lengthy discussions of essential amino acids, protein synthesis, enzyme functions, and vitamin activity. We rely on pet food manufacturers to do our research and formulation. We expect such companies to provide us with analysis and lists of ingredients on the labels so we can make intelligent selections based upon palatability and the best nutritional value for our investment. For these reasons, this discussion of brood animals' dietary needs will go right to the heart of the subject in what should and should not be fed, how much is needed, and why certain foods may be used, and others avoided.

If you want more information, a thorough scientific study of cat nutrition is found in the book *Nutrient Requirements of Cats (Revised)*, available from the National Research Council 1-800-624-6242.

Water

Water is essential to sustain life. (*Nutrient Requirements of Cats* devotes a great deal of space to the subject of water.) The nonfat component of mammalian bodies is about 73 percent water. It is metabolically available from liquids and solid foods. Canned cat food, for example, is 72 to 78 percent water. Smaller quantities of water are also supplied in semimoist diets that contain 25 to 35 percent, and appreciably less water is found in dry cat foods that are 7 to 12 percent moisture.

Significant quantities of oxidation water are produced within an animal's body by catabolism of carbohydrates, fats, and protein. Cats will typically drink water about the same number of times a day as they eat, and they are very efficient in conserving water. If necessary, they can maintain normal health in the total absence of drinking water when fed high moisture diets—but don't rely on it. A constant source of water is extremely important in all cats' diets. The additional stresses of reproduction makes water intake even more critical in breeding queens during all stages of their estrous cycles.

Water is lost from the bodies of cats through their urine and feces. More is lost by evaporation from their respiratory tracts, mucous membranes of the eyes and mouth, and skin. Cats lose great amounts of water during illnesses, especially when they are suffering from digestive problems accompanied by diarrhea or vomiting. Lost water must be replaced constantly. Cats, like all intelligent beings, prefer fresh, clean drinking water.

Feeding Brood Stock

The cousins of house cats, including lions and tigers, practice a

A sable Burmese.

feast and famine feeding program. They will gorge on their kill until they can hold no more, and they hunt again when hunger drives them to do so. Not so for cunning house cats. They are individuals by every definition of the word, but they have one thing in common: When a complete and balanced diet is offered, they will generally stop eating when their daily nutritional requirements are met. They are masters of the art of nibbling and snacking. Eating a dozen or more snacks a day, they only engorge themselves if given access to large quantities of highly palatable foods.

Weigh each of your cats occasionally. Young, athletic animals are often heavier than they appear to be, due to their solid musculature and lack of soft fat. Adult cats require between 28 and 40 k/cal of energy per pound of body weight per day, which means that a 10 pound (4.5 kg) adult cat should consume about 300 to 400 k/cal daily for mainte-

Burmese in a basket.

the price of a cat food does not necessarily reflect the nutritional value of the product. Packaging and advertising are included in the price. Try not to base your cat food selections on the cute kitten pictures on the product label. Don't make your purchase from information received on TV commercials featuring healthy, beautiful cats. Remember those animals are paid actors, and they have little to say about what they are fed.

The cost of each element used to produce a food that meets or exceeds your pet's daily requirements affects the price of pet foods. That's one reason why today's premium cat foods sit on one end of the price scale, and the generic foods on the other. Many excellent quality premium foods are rarely if ever advertised on television.

As is the case with most other manufactured food products, when you shop for cat food, you will usually get about what you pay for unless you buy a lot of advertising. Your breeding cat's nutrition is a poor place to try to balance your household budget. House brands and generic packages may contain balanced nutrition, but their contents and palatability may vary as the prices of ingredients increase or decrease. It is also possible that a house brand may be identical to a brand-name product. Personal contact with manufacturers is the best way to obtain that information. Their addresses and phone numbers are usually easy to find on the packages.

nance. (See Glossary, page 152, for the definition of k/cal.)

An energetic cat that climbs, plays, and exercises frequently requires one fourth to one third more energy than one that is older and less active. More is said about specific dietary needs during pregnancy (Chapter 6) and lactation (Chapter 10).

A discussion of caloric sources and costs is a useless academic exercise. The wide range of k/cal per ounce of the hundreds of cat foods presently available is mind-boggling, and the price range is equally broad. An important fact to remember is that

Types of Cat Foods

The three types of prepared cat foods are dry, semimoist, and canned. Protein digestibility ranges from 80 percent in dry cat foods to 85 percent in semimoist and 90 percent in canned meat diets. Canned foods are usually about three fourths water. Even though they contain meat, their formula may indicate only 10 percent protein, whereas a dry food with little or no animal products (meat) may contain 35 percent protein by dry weight. Those figures are influenced by the water content of the food.

Dry food is less energy-dense and less palatable than canned products, but it has advantages that the other types do not share. It can be left unrefrigerated for free-choice feeding. It is cleaner, has less odor, is easier to handle, and usually costs less than the other two types.

Semimoist foods contain preservatives to help prevent spoilage, and other elements are added to bind water. These foods are expensive, and feeding them frequently stimulates a significant increase in water consumption due to the chemical additives.

Canned foods come in two varieties: *Rations*, which contain soy, cereal, meat, vitamins, and minerals; and *gourmet* foods that contain more meat, vitamins and minerals, and less vegetable matter. Although a small rodent represents a balanced meal for a cat, a mouse is not all meat. By the same measure, diets composed of 100 percent beef, pork, poultry, or fish are not nutritionally balanced. Higher priced ingredients and supplements are included in canned formulations making them expensive by comparison to dry foods. If the correct quantities are fed, however, spoilage is not a problem, because there should be no leftovers.

Cats have no actual fat requirement for energy. They can obtain all their energy from protein and carbohydrates. Fats add palatability to a food and some fat is needed for proper metabolism of fat-soluble vitamins (A, D, E, and K). Dry foods are lowest in fat; canned foods are highest. The range is from 9 percent to 20 percent. Wild felines' natural diets probably contain 40 percent fat, or even more, but that doesn't mean you should add fat to the prepared diet of your house cat.

In the past there was some fear of all cat foods, especially dry rations, because of their high mineral content that was believed to cause feline urological syndrome (FUS) (see Noncontagious Diseases, page 136). Research has shed much light on that disease, and today most premium cat foods of all three types contain carefully balanced minerals. Several products are specially formulated to minimize FUS risk and maintain an acidic urine production. Of the three types of food available, specially formulated premium canned varieties are probably the food of choice for prevention of FUS.

Premium brands of cat foods use a fixed formula that remains constant,

Maine coon cat.

Each label is a legal document. If you want detailed information about cat food labels, you can obtain a pamphlet (for a fee) from the Association of American Feed Control Officials (AAFCO) by calling 1-404-656-3637.

Some labels carry the important statement: *"Provides complete and balanced nutrition for the growth and maintenance of cats as substantiated through testing in accordance with AAFCO feeding protocols."* Take special note of that statement. When it is seen, the product can be fed as the only source of nutrition for kittens and adult breeding cats. Certain food labels will state that the food is formulated for all life stages of cats. That, too, is important, but should be taken seriously only if it is substantiated in feeding trials.

If you want more information about the food, such as how the analysis was made, call or write to the manufacturer. The most valid analysis is obtained by animal feeding tests. That is because a laboratory analysis to establish compliance with AAFCO regulations does not necessarily address nutrient excesses, unmeasured toxic substances, or palatability.

Homemade diets: Recipes for home-formulated diets are available in health food stores and libraries, and *Nutrient Requirements of Cats* gives some guidelines for formulating diets from natural ingredients. Homemade diets should be avoided unless you can be sure of the protein, fat, and carbohydrate content, and the digestibility of every ingredient.

even when the market costs of ingredients change. Some other less expensive foods use a least cost formula that results in variations in the ingredients used, as the market prices of those ingredients fluctuate. Lower cost ingredients can be substituted for others without changing the percentages of fat, carbohydrate, and protein. Unfortunately, unless the label displays specific ingredients, you can't be sure what is contained in the package.

Labels can be misleading. When reading labels, always base your analysis on the *dry matter* weight.

Storage

The age or shelf life of a product is another important consideration, especially in dry and semimoist products. After excessive storage time, either at home or in a store, some elements such as fats and vitamins, may be lost or rendered less nutritionally effective. For that reason, choose products that enjoy popularity among the cat owning public. For the same reason, purchase your cat's food from a busy store that has a high product turnover.

Supplements and Treats

There is no reason to supplement a cat's complete and balanced diet, but if you're like most cat lovers, you will probably treat your feline friend to something special once in a while. In moderation, your cat won't be harmed by an occasional treat. Take care not to furnish more than 20 percent of its energy needs in the treats that you offer.

Many cats enjoy cooked eggs as treats, but you should never feed raw eggs. Egg yolks are very high in fat and, if fed raw, may cause diarrhea. The albumin of raw egg whites interferes with utilization of biotin, a B-complex vitamin. The safest cat treats are bits of well-cooked meat such as chicken, turkey, beef, or fish, always fed in small quantities. A better idea is to occasionally change the flavor of the premium canned food you are using. Your feline buddy will appreciate something new now and then, and its diet will remain complete and balanced.

Supplements should be added to food only if approved by your veterinarian.

What Not to Feed

Table scraps, no matter how tempting, should never be substituted for cat food. Feeding table scraps will stimulate nuisance behavior of cats when you are preparing or eating your meals. Table scraps are not complete and balanced nutrition for cats. Human food seasonings and preservatives, such as benzoic acid, may be toxic to your cat. It is speculated that propylene glycol, used to control water activity in some processed human foods, may be detrimental to feline red blood cells.

Raw fish can be harmful. In large quantities, it may cause vitamin E deficiency in cats. Commercial feline diets containing fish are typically supplemented with vitamin E. Products like canned tuna sold for human consumption are not complete, balanced diets for cats, and should not be used as a significant part of your cat's daily nutrition.

Milk should never be included in a feline diet. It is dangerous, even when fed in small quantities. Adult cats are usually deficient in lactase, the enzyme that digests lactose sugar in milk. The composition of cow's milk is significantly different from cat's milk. For these reasons, when milk is fed to kittens (and many adult cats), it will often cause diarrhea. Vomiting or diarrhea results in dehydration, reduced physical activity, weight loss, malnourishment, and depression.

Liver contains high levels of vitamin A that may cause problems in any cat, especially kittens. It is also a laxative and is a very poorly balanced food.

Candy: Why anyone would feed candy to a cat is beyond comprehension, but in case you are thinking of it, don't! Most cats have no sweet tooth. They don't need sugar or nuts, and certainly not cocoa, which can be toxic to cats.

Balanced vitamin and mineral supplements may not be harmful, but if you are feeding a complete and balanced diet, they are a waste of money and add nothing to the cat's nutrition. Speak to your veterinarian before you add vitamins or minerals to your cat's diet.

Feeding Advice:
The Bottom Line

Television promotions would like pet owners to believe that all cats' palates are quite sensitive. They promote the idea that only particular brands of food satisfy those delicate taste buds. Mostly, that isn't true. Cats aren't born with finicky appetites, but owners often create fussy eaters with inappropriate feeding programs. If you rush out and buy a new flavored food every time your feline partner skips a meal, the result is bound to be a finicky appetite. Cats typically consume only the calories they require. If they are inactive, they may skip a meal or two.

Personally, I prefer to offer dry cat food free-choice, around the clock. If that feeding system is begun while your pet is still a growing kitten, there is usually little problem with engorging. The cat will become accustomed to having the food there whenever a quick snack is desired, and, in my experience, few cats become obese from over-consumption of dry cat food that is fed free-choice. Naturally that feeding plan may not work if your household includes other animals that rob the cat food bowl. In our home, we feed the cat(s) on top of a counter that is inaccessible to dogs.

Cats usually prefer their canned food at room temperature, not straight from the refrigerator. I have heard reports of cats refusing foods that were warmed in microwave ovens, but in our home that is not a problem. You may feed your feline roommate regular meals of canned food twice or three times a day. If you prefer, they can be fed free-choice dry food around-the-clock with no added canned food. Kittens need at least two, and preferably three or four, canned food meals a day if no dry food is available to them. Because of contamination from insects, I caution you not to leave canned food at room temperature for more than an hour. If it isn't quickly eaten, pick it up, seal it in a plastic container, and put it back into the refrigerator.

An excellent and economical feeding plan for adult cats is to purchase small packages of premium dry foods. In addition to the free-choice dry food, offer half of a 6-ounce can of premium quality canned food each morning and evening for variety. Be sure that both the dry and canned foods contain the AAFCO feeding trial nutritional statement.

A 9- or 10-pound (4.1–4.5 kg) cat will maintain nicely on approximately ½ cup of dry food and one 6-ounce can of food a day, getting about half of its daily nutritional requirements from each of those two sources. That combination should furnish about 300 k/cal per day (see specific feeding recommendations for pregnant and lactating queens, Chapters 6 and 10, and kittens, Chapters 12).

There is no reason to change brands of food periodically. It is best to find one or two that agree with both your cat and your purse, and stay with them. If you decide to change brands of food, it won't interfere with the cat's nutrition, providing that the change is made gradually, and the food quality is maintained. Sudden changes often cause digestive upsets, so always add the new food to the former product in increasing amounts, over a period of several days, while gradually reducing the former food.

Premium brands: From the standpoint of the National Research Council's (NRC) requirements, analysis, and compliance with AAFCO labeling, there is no particular reason for paying high prices for premium foods. The increased cost of premium diets probably can't be justified when their formulas are compared to the formulas of excellent quality brandname products found in grocery stores. However, when premium foods are fed regularly, you might find that your cat simply looks better. It may better maintain its condition during the stresses of breeding, pregnancy, and lactation. If you are keeping a cat that is not in a breeding program, perhaps a feeding trial is in order, using your cat as the participant.

Selection of brands: Try feeding a specific grocery store cat food for three or four months. Keep a record of the cost of the food, not the quantity eaten, during a period of 90 days. Then gradually change to a specific premium food that is purchased from a pet supply store or

This is supposed to be fun.

from your veterinarian. Record the cost of the premium food eaten over an equal period of time. Note which food the cat preferred, and try to evaluate the cat's condition and appearance. Then make your choice accordingly. Although such a trial may furnish considerable knowledge, I do not recommend it for animals in breeding programs. For them, it is best to choose a premium brand and stay with it.

Fat Cats

Obesity is not usually a problem in breeding animals, but when it occurs, it reduces reproductive potential. If your queen gains too much weight between litters, stop free-choice feeding and reduce her daily dietary intake by 15 or 20 percent until her weight has been reduced to the optimum. Many brands of cat food also offer a lower calorie diet, specifically formulated to reduce the weight of an obese cat while maintaining the complete and balanced formulation. Such foods are acceptable for pets, but you should not feed those calorie-restricted reducing diets to breeding queens during their active reproductive cycles.

Avail yourself of the information that manufacturers will furnish about their foods. Write or call the producers of pet foods for specific analytic and feeding trial results. You will be amazed how much you can learn by comparing the various products by criteria other than the shelf price. The addresses and (sometimes toll-free) telephone numbers are on pet food packages. Use them.

Government Regulations

Questions are often asked about government regulations imposed on the pet food industry. There are rules

Now this is the life.

and regulations too numerous to detail, but a brief discussion is in order.

- The U.S. Food and Drug Administration (FDA) regulates quality controls in the manufacture of canned foods, food additives, and product labeling. It sets label standards regarding the predominance of ingredients; those ingredients must be listed by weight in descending order. If water is the first ingredient listed, it is the predominant part of the product. If the next ingredient is wheat, followed by other plant products, you know that they make up the principal parts of the product. The FDA also requires certain terminology standards. For instance, if a product is labeled beef, it must contain 95 percent *beef*. If it is labeled *all beef*, it means the total content is beef.

  The FDA also requires additives to meet *Generally Recognized As Safe* (GRAS) standards. This regulation protects consumers from purchasing products containing elements that have not been previously used with safety. Finally, the FDA has a *Good Manufacturing Practice* (GMP) standard. That regulation requires all manufacturing companies to adhere to standards of production equal to the rest of the industry.

- The Association of American Feed Control Officials (AAFCO) is a national organization of state officials. Their principal function is to provide testing requirements and protocols for manufacturers. They require veterinarian examination of all test animals, and evaluation of testing is done by qualified veterinarians and animal nutritionists. The AAFCO also requires each label to contain a guaranteed analysis of minimum percentage of protein, fat, and carbohydrate.

- The Federal Trade Commission (FTC) is responsible for monitoring and enforcing advertising claims, truth in advertising, and other manufacturing and marketing functions.

- The Environmental Protection Agency (EPA) establishes the maximum permitted levels and tolerances for pesticides and other chemicals that might be found in the products.

- The National Research Council of the National Academy of Sciences (NRC) reviews scientific literature regarding minimum nutritional needs. They publish the information and disseminate it to the public as well as the pet food industry. They play a vital advisory role for pet owners.

- Finally, the United States Department of Agriculture (USDA) regulates the four Ds of pet foods—dead, dying, diseased, and disabled—representing animal products used in pet foods. The source of all animal products must be identified by a manufacturer, and if any is obtained from animals in those categories, USDA regulations require the products to be rendered at high temperatures to kill all harmful bacteria and viruses. Knowing that the meat in your prize queen's favorite canned cat food came from one of those sources may offend you. Try not to dwell on it. You can't tell from the label what the meat source was, but most premium pet-food meat doesn't originate from the four D categories. It is usually obtained as fresh meat and is carefully handled under strictly controlled conditions.

Health and Immune Status

The general health of a breeding animal includes more than its nutritional state. Your veterinarian's physical examination and laboratory tests assured you of the cat's health at the time the queen was purchased. That was an excellent beginning, but ongoing health maintenance and preventive medicine are equally important.

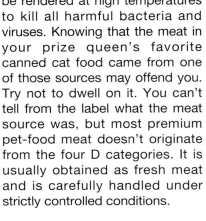

Vaccinations are an important part of a successful cat-breeding operation.

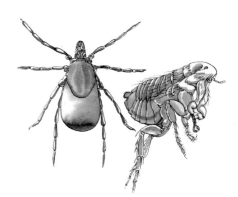

Adult fleas and ticks cause skin irritation.

Fecal specimens should be collected and taken to your veterinarian prior to each breeding or at least once a year. Generally it isn't necessary to repeat blood tests if the queen is not exposed to other cats. If she is taken to another cattery for breeding or is boarded in a kennel, annual blood testing might be prudent. There are no safe generalities to make regarding blood testing. One or more of the several available tests may be advised in one part of the country, and not in other places, depending on the prevalence of diseases.

Choosing the right queen to breed is no more critical than a well-designed immunization program. Vaccinations are as essential as good nutrition in a feline breeding program. (Feline diseases, and their prevention through vaccination, are covered in detail in Chapter 14.) Annual vaccinations should be scheduled for about the time the queen is bred so as to obtain the highest possible level of immunity when the kittens are born.

Because a queen's antibodies do not appreciably cross the placental barrier to enter the bloodstream of the fetuses, kittens arrive in the world with very little disease resistance. They obtain antibodies and disease protection from their dam's colostral milk. This first milk provides a passive immunity that will last until they are old enough to develop their own active immunity through vaccinations. By vaccinating a queen shortly before she is bred, her circulating antibody level is at its peak at queening time, when her colostral milk is produced.

Stud Cat Selection

Toms aren't usually kept in small catteries, but if you can afford to own and care for a male of exceptional quality, you might consider buying one. You should be aware, though, of several problems inherent in owning a tom. In addition to the odor and undesirable habits of breeding males, there is the genetic problem. If your queen produces occasional female kittens of exceptional quality, you will probably decide to keep them, to strengthen your bloodline and to replace your aging queen when her reproductive years are spent. You can't consider breeding a young queen to her father, so you must locate another stud. You are back at square one.

Locating a stud to use shouldn't be an insurmountable task. By the time one is needed you will have acquired many feline-owning friends from cat shows, clubs, and newsletters. The best source for a tom will probably be advertisements in a cat fancy magazine or a breed newsletter. Look at the prospective studs, compare them with the breed standards, and be sure their faults are not the same as those found in your queen. Handle the studs personally. If their temperaments do not allow handling, they probably shouldn't contribute to the gene pool of your bloodline. Make your selection after considering as many males as possible.

A future stud? This lynx point Himalayan kitten won CFA's "3rd Best Kitten" award for 1995–96.

Don't ship your queen across the country to an animal you have never seen unless you have personal knowledge of his temperament and conformation quality. Don't catalog shop! If possible, handle and examine the stud's offspring from queens that are related to your cat.

Stud Fees

Stud fees should be written into breeding contracts. They are usually negotiated between the two animal owners, and depend on many factors. Fees should be based on the quality of offspring of a tom. Many high-winning males are not great producers. Conversely, if the tom in question has produced a couple of dozen champion kittens, his fee should be expected to be rather steep. If you decide to use an inexperienced tom, his parents and siblings should be carefully evaluated. The fee for a young tom's service should be considerably lower than that of a proven male.

Once a fee is decided upon, consideration must be given to return services in the unlikely event that your queen doesn't conceive. That concept should also be included in the breeding contract. If the queen is a proven show winner and has produced excellent kittens in the past, the stud fee might include a choice kitten from the litter, with a considerably lower monetary charge. Most importantly, when an agreement is reached, reduce its every facet to a written document. Don't depend on a handshake or a telephone conversation to seal and bind the deal. Even if the stud is owned by a close friend, treat this part of cat breeding in a purely businesslike manner. Local and national breed clubs and some cat registries can furnish samples of breeding contracts. Use them!

Chapter 3
When to Breed

Seasonality of Estrus

Estrous (spelled with an "o") cycles refer to the changing phenomena of the hormonal and reproductive systems of mammals from the beginning of one estrus (heat) period to the beginning of the next. The term *heat* is synonymous with estrus, spelled without an "o." *Estrus* is one of the four phases of the *estrous* cycle. A queen is said to be in season, in estrus, or in heat when she displays the physical and hormonal signs indicating her acceptance of a male, ovulation, and conception.

Intact refers to a male or female cat that has not been surgically altered to remove its reproductive capacity. Many terms are used in reference to surgical sterilization of cats. *Altered, castrated, fixed, neutered*, and others refer to removal of both testicles of a tom. Female sterilization is usually accomplished by removal of both ovaries and the uterus. Such an operation is properly called *spaying*, but many also use terms like fixed, neutered, or altered.

Another term used frequently is *feral*. Feral usually refers to undomesticated animals. In this book, the definition has been broadened slightly to include feline colonies or individual cats that descended from domestic house cats, but have adopted a lifestyle that doesn't include human interface. In other words, they are the progeny of former house pets that now live in a semi-wild culture of their own. They include ranch cats that roam fields and farm outbuildings, living on rodents and raising their young in sheds or old straw stacks.

Suburban and urban feral cats are very obvious to careful observers as well. They may be seen scavenging in dumpsters and restaurant garbage cans, reproducing in or under abandoned buildings, sheds, culverts or other small, accessible places of refuge. Estrous cycles of feral cats may differ considerably from those of house cats.

The feline estrous cycle (see page 40) is composed of periods or phases called proestrus, estrus, diestrus, and anestrus.

Cats are said by some researchers to be *seasonally polyestrous,* meaning that their estrous cycles are multiple annually, but are affected by climatic conditions or seasons of the year. To a degree, that is correct, but there is much more to the estrous story of felines.

Typically, queens exhibit physical signs of heat about every three weeks until they are bred. Because they exhibit signs of heat for about a week, a favorite expression of mine is that "queens over six months old are either in heat, pregnant, or spayed."

Cats' estrous cycles are said to be photoperiod-dependent. That translates to their propensity to cease cycling during the short days of the late fall and early winter months. Genetics may also affect feline estrous cycles. Some investigators make an excellent argument that shorthair cats are more apt to cycle without notable interruption year-round, whereas the cycles of longhairs tend to be influenced by seasons. Unfortunately, you can't depend on that. Most domestic cats tend to reside indoors during the short days of winter, thereby exposing themselves to extended artificial light hours.

The estrous cycles of feral or free-ranging pet cats conform more closely to the academic descriptions of feline seasonal cyclicity. Their estrous cycles are somewhat similar to those of their wild cousins, such as Asian leopard cats. Because the stewardship practice of confining pets to one's home to reduce the overabundance of homeless animals is encouraged, this book primarily addresses indoor cats.

In my experience, house cats may show some slight reduction in estrous cycle activity during November, December, and January, but I have helped deliver many litters of January and February kittens. In other words, don't depend on the short days of the cold season of the year to keep your queen out of heat.

Feral cats usually only raise one or two litters a year, but cats in homes where they are exposed to about 12 hours of light daily, may raise three litters if mated at every opportunity. If you keep a breeding queen in your home, you may wish to attempt to stop her estrus behavior by controlling her exposure to light during the winter months. That might mean confining her away from all artificial light for several months. If she is kept in a room without artificial light during the evening and early morning hours every day, she may not cycle during those months. Don't bet the farm on it!

Puberty

In normal nutritional and health status, queens reach sexual maturity between five and twelve months of age. The age of puberty is also subject to seasonality to a degree. Feral queens that are born during the summer months often do not show their first signs of estrus until the following early spring, when seven to nine months old. Those that are born in April may come into their first heat at five or six months of age.

As you might expect, house cats do not follow the academic seasonal guidelines that apply to feral cats. When raised in homes, queens often reach puberty and come in heat at five or six months, regardless of the season of their birth.

Puberty may also be induced to a degree. Increasing the hours of light to which a young queen is exposed seems to hasten the onset of estrus. Exposure to other cycling queens and to breeding toms also tend to stimulate earlier puberty.

Best Breeding Age

Unfortunately, queens in heat will usually mate and conceive when they are bred, regardless of their age or the season of the year. A cat is rarely mature by five or six months old, so common sense dictates that you wait until she is fully developed before you allow her to be bred. By a year old, most queens are ready to take on the responsibility of a family. In most cases, queens can be safely bred during any heat period after reaching one year of age.

There are exceptions to every general rule. If a queen has any health or nutritional problems, wait until they are corrected. If she has a temperament deficiency, don't breed her until she is conditioned, trained, and the disposition problem is solved. If she demonstrates a bad attitude in spite of training, don't

Pair of colorpoint Siamese kittens.

breed her at all! Personality traits are partially inherited, and ornery cats aren't in great demand.

Consider your own plans as well as the health and condition of the queen. Look ahead nine weeks and choose a breeding time to produce kittens when it is convenient for you to spend considerable time with them. Remember, your queen will be in heat again every ten to twenty days, giving you ample opportunity to manage the breeding program to your advantage.

The optimal breeding life span for most queens is approximately five years, although many continue to produce kittens much longer if allowed. Queens often produce a small litter the first time bred, then the number of kittens increases to normal (four to six) during the rest of her productive life. Litter size and kitten vitality deteriorate as a queen reaches six or seven years of age. With proper management, two litters a year can be produced for several years without undue stress on a queen. That means a soundly managed, healthy queen can produce up to 50 kittens during her prime reproductive years, and even more if allowed. There is, however, some doubt in my mind about the rationality of pushing kitten production to that level considering today's overpopulation problems.

I suggest you consider resting the queen for six months after two litters. Begin the resting period when the second litter is weaned, and after a couple of more litters, rest her again. I believe the quality of kittens produced and the health of the queen will more than compensate for the reproductive time lost.

Kitten production should address more than the health of the dam (mother). As a breeder, you also have the responsibility to place your kittens in good, loving homes. I advise that all cat breeding programs receive careful study and at least a semiannual review. Revisions in your program should be based on the quality of kittens produced in the last litter, the health and disposition of the dam, and the market. If excellent homes are dwindling, perhaps the kitten supply is too great.

Sexual Maturity and Habits of Toms

Most toms begin to show early signs of puberty and sexual interest by six or seven months of age. One of the first indications that a tom is thinking of romance is when he takes a "neck grasp" on another cat (see photo, page 59). The object of this physical act may be a breeding queen, a spayed female, or even a neutered tom. That singular sign doesn't mean he is capable of consummating the breeding act, nor that his semen contains viable sperm. It does warn owners that it is time to consider his future. If he is not to be included in your breeding program, he has reached the age to schedule a castration appointment

Tomcats typically reach breeding age by about nine or ten months, although I've known precocious toms that sired normal litters of kittens at six months. As they mature, the lives of intact toms are driven by a reproductive urge. Every adult tom seems determined to take sole responsibility for the propagation of the feline species. Feral toms are unusually energetic and resourceful breeders. They challenge other males, seek out females, leave scented messages for them, and make repeated journeys to the homes of females.

Intact queens make fine house pets, usually tolerating other pets quite well and causing no problems except when they are in heat. That is not the case with toms however; they require special attention and usually spend most of their lives confined to kennels for several compelling reasons.

Intact adult males are predisposed to make their presence known to prospective mates. When a female in heat echoes forth her mating calls, toms answer. Even a queen calling from down the street will stimulate loud tomcat responses of a most unmelodious and distasteful nature. Besides their vocal din, their sexual signaling systems use urine as another communication medium. Amorous males spray their endless urine supply on various objects throughout their territory to announce their availability. It is an open invitation to roaming queens in heat, serving to announce the presence of a breeding tom in the neighborhood. Feral queens recognize the odor, and to find mates, they need only make themselves known with a few calls.

Tomcat urine has a distinctive odor all its own. It is terribly pungent, foul, and disagreeable in nature. When marking their territory, a feral tom's urine isn't deposited in a hole in the earth and covered up. Instead, it is sprayed on vertical surfaces such as trees, corners of buildings, haystacks, shrubs, and about every other inanimate object you can imagine.

All toms are territorial, and they will aggressively defend their marked area against intruding toms. Besides announcing their presence to interested queens, the urine odor serves as a territorial warning to other toms that might venture by. The most common cat injuries in our practice were related to cat fights, most of which involved two or more toms defending their breeding territories.

It is a pity that indoor toms don't realize that territory marking isn't necessary inside their own houses. Unfortunately, they also mark their territory with odious, offensive urine. They back up to chairs, drapes, clothes hanging in a closet, doors, and virtually any other vertical surfaces, and, with a twitching tail, spray away. When soaked into upholstery, the urine stench remains indefinitely. Indoor spraying is usually intolerable behavior, but it can't be corrected, so the tom is confined to a kennel most of the time.

The Queen's Reproductive Anatomy

The reproductive anatomy of queens includes two ovaries that reside near the kidneys in the upper mid-abdomen (see illustration, page 40). Each is enclosed in a sort of capsule that acts as a funnel leading to openings into the Fallopian tubes (oviducts). The Fallopian tubes lie folded against the sides of both ovaries and reach to the tips of the uterine horns, serving as transport channels for ova between the ovaries and the uterus.

The uterus of many domestic mammals including the feline, is a Y-shaped organ. The arms of the Y are called *uterine horns*, and the posterior, lower portion is termed the *uterine body*. The uterine body terminates as a constriction called the *cervix,* which joins with the forward portion of the *vagina*. The vagina

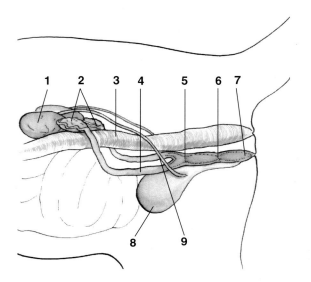

Female genitalia. 1 = Left kidney,
2 = Ovaries, 3 = Colon, 4 = Left uterine horn,
5 = Uterine body, 6 = Cervix, 7 = Vagina,
8 = Urinary bladder, 9 = Left ureter.

ends in the outermost portion of the reproductive tract, which is called the *vulva*.

The *uterine vault* (cavity within the uterus) is lined with specialized tissues that promote embryonic attachment and growth. The contiguous vagina and vulva are accessible from the outside and the vagina serves as a receptacle for a tom's sperm at the time of breeding.

Feline-Canine Estrous Differences

The above anatomical description might fit several mammalian species, including canines. A major difference between canine and feline

reproductive systems lies in the physical signs of proestrus. Bitches undergo several obvious changes that are lacking in queens. The vulvas of canines swell and become flaccid, and considerable bloody discharge emerges from the genital tract during proestrus and early estrus. Neither the physical changes nor the discharge are seen in queens.

Feline Estrous Cycle

Proestrus is the first recognizable phase of feline estrous cycles. It lasts only a day or two, but is not likely to go unnoticed by owners. Queens experiencing proestrus hormone changes first become more sociable with their human friends. They desire more petting, and rub their bodies along their owners' legs, seeking attention. They play less, and their appetites usually wane slightly. Then they begin acting so strangely that many novice cat breeders call their veterinarians, believing their queens to be quite ill.

During my years of veterinary practice, I received hundreds of non-emergency telephone calls in the middle of the night from owners of pubescent queens. The dynamic feline estrus antics take many forms, including rolling about on the floor, rubbing their faces on the floor, and standing with their hind ends elevated while holding their faces to the floor.

Queens in proestrus usually pedal with their hind feet, holding their backs arched downward. When you begin to pet them, their tails are held aside, their elbows lie flat on the carpet, and their derrieres are elevated. Often they emit low moans with each petting stroke. Although they delight in petting, they usually aren't interested in quiet lap sitting.

These queens become aggressively interested in finding mates. They will watch for opportunities to escape from your home, and throwing caution to the winds, they strike off in search of a breeding age tom. Usually mates aren't difficult to locate!

Vocalization is pronounced, often to extremes. Eerie sounds of yowling, deep-throated growling, and high-pitched screams are common. We once owned a Siamese queen that sounded like a cat from hell during proestrus. Our neighbors actually called to see if one of our children was injured. Her yowls precluded sleeping in the same house with her. Needless to say, she was promptly spayed.

Many unwanted kittens are the result of owners misunderstanding the significance of a queen's first proestrus. When she begins her weird antics, the naive owners open the back door. The proestrus queen disappears for a day or two, then returns in her former, loving, quiet mood. Nine weeks later, the owners are several kittens richer.

Toms are certainly attracted to queens during proestrus, but copulation doesn't take place until the

A queen in estrus frequently assumes strange postures.

next phase (estrus) begins. Mood swings are dynamic as queens become more friendly toward intact males. *Intromission* (the successful and complete entry of a tom's penis into a queen's vagina) is not allowed in early proestrus, however, and the queen usually folds her tail between her hind legs to prevent completion of the breeding act.

Proestrus Hormonal Changes

Proestrus is prompted by follicle stimulating hormone (FSH) that originates in the pituitary gland. That

Sally in the sink.

hormone's target organs are the ovaries, and its effect is to stimulate production of ovarian follicles. Within those follicles, ova (eggs) are generated. Ova mature quickly and are released into the oviducts at the time of ovulation. An estrogenic hormone (Estradiol 17ß) is produced in the follicles as well. It is the influence of estrogens that causes the queen's erratic (or erotic) behavioral attitudes that dominate proestrus and early estrus.

Estrus

Estrus is the second phase of the estrous cycle. It is outwardly differentiated from proestrus by the fact that a queen will allow a male to mount. Intromission then takes place and the breeding act is accomplished.

Estrus lasts up to ten days if a queen is not bred, and only three or four days if coitus is accomplished. Those time periods vary slightly from queen to queen. Queens are receptive to males throughout the estrus period. The physical breeding act (copulation), initiates the release of lutenizing hormone (LH) from the pituitary gland, and LH stimulates ovulation. That characteristic is not unique to the cat (coitus-induced ovulation is also seen in rabbits), but it is quite different from the reproductive physiology of most other domestic animals, and is worthy of discussion.

In order to produce LH from the pituitary gland, a certain level of copulatory stimulus must be reached. The duration and magnitude of LH levels seem to vary according to the individual cat. The LH surge that results from mating is responsible for causing ovulation. Sufficient stimulation and LH surge may follow a single mating in some queens, but not in others. It has been shown that the level of LH increases with repeated copulatory activities. It is obvious that induced ovulation, coupled with the frequency of estrus (every two or three weeks), enhances the reproductive capacity of felines, and increases homeless cat populations.

Another seemingly important aspect of naturally induced ovulation pertains to the morphology of the feline penis (see illustration, page 57) Papillae, or small spiny projections, cover the surface of the feline glans penis. It is often postulated that the rough, prickly covering of that organ is important to provide sufficient copulatory stimulus for the production of effective levels of LH.

As LH levels rise following ovulation, the estrus period concludes and corpora lutea form. A *corpus luteum* (singular) is a yellowish, scar-like body left in the ovary after an ovarian follicle ruptures and an ovum is released. Late in the estrus period another hormone, called *progesterone*, is secreted by corpora lutea.

Logical breeding time: Research veterinarians have observed feline ovulation through a *laparoscope,* which is a fiber-optic instrument introduced into the abdomen through a tiny incision. It is reported

*An artistocratic
Persian cat.*

that when queens are mated three times daily at four-hour intervals for three consecutive days (or for the duration of estrus), ovulation occurs late on the third or early on the fourth day of estrus. That confirms the rationale of breeding a queen for three consecutive days to stimulate ovulation and attain pregnancy.

Estrus terminates shortly after breeding, but there is ample time for a queen on the street to be bred and to produce kittens from more than one male. Many successful cat breeders leave a tom and queen together as long as she will periodically allow the male to mount. Allowing more than one male to mate with a queen is obviously poor breeding management and should be avoided.

Although the mating behavior of most queens leaves little doubt about what phase of the estrous

cycle she is experiencing, there are laboratory tools that can be used to monitor breeding programs. Hormone assays are possible, but they are not as easily interpreted as in canines. The problems encountered with feline laboratory assay data relates to the brief duration of proestrus and estrus phases. Hormone levels seem to vary considerably between individual queens, and establishing normal comparative values is difficult. Feline serum hormone values continue to be studied, and more information is available each year. When problem breeders are identified, I recommend that you consult a feline reproductive specialist.

Vaginal cytology: Vaginal smears may be made by gathering cells from the vestibule or vaginal vault with a special sterile medicine dropper. From the vaginal-wash fluid obtained, microscope slides are prepared, and the tissue cells found are specially stained. Those cells aid in identifying proestrus or estrus phases. The technique is not difficult, but it is usually only indicated in cases of silent heats, which are indeed very rare in felines. It is one of the first examinations to perform if a healthy queen fails to cycle normally.

A possible adverse side effect from collecting vaginal cells deserves mention. The technique involves flushing a few drops of sterile saline solution into the vestibule and vagina with a special blunt medicine dropper. Then, several drops of the fluid are captured with the dropper as it flushes out. Unfortunately, if the queen is experiencing a normal estrus period, the medicine dropper manipulation may stimulate an LH surge and subsequent ovulation. In other words, it is a good idea to have your stud cat on standby in case estrus is identified. Immediate breeding may be advised.

Artificially induced estrus: Rarely is there need or desire to artificially stimulate a queen's estrus activities, but occasionally a valuable breeding animal remains in anestrus. When queens do not apparently cycle, a series of injections of FSH may be administered that will usually result in estrus activities. The dosage and frequency is critical, and the procedure should only be used by experienced veterinarians. Misuse may result in additional physiological problems.

Another technique for estrus induction uses another hormone, PMSG (pregnant mares' serum gonadotropin), but again, misuse can be disastrous. Safety and efficacy must be considered. There is little documented conclusive data to support the artificial stimulation of estrus and ovulation, except in rare situations. In my experience, the overall health, nutritional status, and stress of breeding queens should be carefully evaluated before deciding to use chemical stimulation of estrus.

Estrus prevention: The only safe, proven method to interrupt the feline estrous cycle and prevent estrus and its undesirable behavior is surgical spaying. Removal of the uterus and ovaries is permanent, and can't be reversed. In the hands of a competent veterinary surgeon, it is safe, and reliable, and recuperation is rapid and uneventful.

Numerous chemical techniques are available to stop estrus activity temporarily, but I can't personally support any of them. Various progesterone-like hormones may be administered orally or by injection. Some have a duration of activity of two months; others may delay estrus longer. I believe they share a health safety risk that precludes their use, including their deleterious effect on the uterus. I have also read of instances wherein diabetes was thought to be associated with the use of those progesterone products.

Diestrus

The third phase of the feline estrous cycle is termed *diestrus* (formerly called *metestrus*). It is usually defined as the period of time during which progesterone hormone activities govern a queen's reproductive cycle. If ovulation takes place, progesterone levels continue to remain elevated throughout pregnancy or false pregnancy. If the queen is not mated, the corpora lutea regress, progesterone levels abate, and soon the queen will begin to show signs of proestrus behavior.

During diestrus, queens reject mating overtures by toms, and their outward behavior returns to normal. This progesterone-dominated phase lasts for the nine-week duration of pregnancy if a queen is bred, or for one or two weeks if ovulation doesn't take place. If ovulation is stimulated without conception, false pregnancy (pseudocyesis) often occurs, in which case diestrus lasts for a month, six weeks, or sometimes longer.

Anestrus

The last phase of an estrous cycle is a resting and recuperative period that occurs between the end of diestrus and the beginning of the next estrus in unmated or nonovulating queens. Called *anestrus*, it is a short period of reproductive inactivity. It is sometimes manifested for several weeks during the short days of winter months if the queen's light exposure is regulated. It is the permanent reproductive condition of spayed females.

During anestrus, queens reject all male amorous advances. Their attitudes are stable, and their activities are normal. Anestrus is a very abbreviated phase in most indoor, intact queens.

Chapter 4
Potential Breeding Problems

If you ask the next person you meet what the most common cat breeding problem is, you will probably receive a dissertation on cat overpopulation. It is true that felines are prolific breeders, and *Felis catus* isn't likely to find its way to the threatened or endangered species list in the near future.

As more purebred cats are produced, more novice breeders are experimenting with linebreeding or inbreeding, and several breeds depend on mutations to propagate their standards. Newly developed and exotic breeds often have a very limited gene pool from which to draw. For these and other reasons, breeding problems are more common in purebred cats than in feral feline communities.

Feral cats that aren't able to breed naturally disappear from the genetic pool in a single generation, thus inherited breeding problems are quickly eliminated from feral populations. Backyard, accidental breeding of house pets may involve breeding problems, but they usually aren't reported, diagnosed, or treated, and are therefore virtually invisible.

In large commercial catteries where colonies of queens are kept in constant contact with one or more toms, breeding problems often go unnoticed or undiagnosed. When a queen fails to produce a litter, she may arbitrarily be retired from the breeding colony without technical investigation or intervention. Poor sanitation, crowding, inter-cat personality conflicts, noise, and respiratory ailments may contribute to such colony breeding problems.

Isolation of New Cats

Some areas of breeding management apply to all operations, regardless of the number of animals involved. One such area is the screening and isolation of newcomers. Seemingly minor respiratory infections, as well as serious diseases, can run rampant among cats, both indoors and outdoors.

On several occasions, I worked with ranch and farm cat populations where normally mild and transitory infections became mortal epidemics.

As contagious diseases weakened the feline population, cats ceased to hunt and lost weight due to poor appetites. Abortions and stillbirths occurred and reproduction stopped. Those rural cat colony problems are usually caused by sick stray cats entering the colony, probably being dumped at the farms by well-meaning people. If unchecked, a usually minor disease can wipe out a feline community. The diseases are very difficult to treat once established, because it is impossible to catch and confine every farm cat for therapy. To prevent problems of that nature in rural populations, large breeding colonies, or carefully controlled small catteries, isolation of all new cats is critically important.

If you plan to acquire a new cat, screen it well. Be sure it is examined by a veterinarian before taking it home. When you take it home, isolate it from your breeding animals for at least ten days. Prevent physical contact, and control aerosol and vector contacts with your other cats. That means keeping the new cat in a separate room, preferably at the opposite end of the house, well away from other cats. There should be no common food or water bowls, and you should wash your hands well after feeding, petting, or handling the new cat. Some feline viral upper respiratory diseases exist in a carrier state in which the infected animal may appear normal, but virus shedding occurs either continuously or intermittently. If outward symptoms of disease do not surface within ten days, it is usually safe to introduce the new cat to the other feline members of the cattery.

If friends ask you to board their pet cat for a few days, don't hesitate to inquire about recent illnesses. If the pet has so much as sniffled or coughed in the past couple of weeks, don't do it! Pet owners often refer to feline upper respiratory infections as "a little cold," but they could cause more trouble than the friendship is worth to you.

Reproductive Stress

Breeding animals are subjected to stresses directly associated with estrus, the breeding act, pregnancy, parturition, and lactation. In other words, normal reproductive activity is stressful. If that stress is increased or aggravated by nutritional imbalances or illnesses, reproductive capacity may be reduced. Appropriate vaccination programs, reproductive rest periods, parasite control, and other factors that may help prevent breeding problems are all important. Personal attention is yet another aspect of preventive medicine.

Cats are individuals, and to get the greatest dividends from your investment in a fine quality breeding queen, you must consider her as a unique animal, with particular needs and desires. I doubt if any queens in large breeding colonies produce the best possible kittens because they are subjected to stresses inherent in

Himalayan kittens.

a large operation. Privacy and individual considerations are precluded by the great numbers of cats in the colony. In household breeding programs, queens can all receive your personal attention. Give them lots of petting, grooming, and lap time!

Silent Heats

Unapparent estrus, or silent heat, is occasionally seen in cats. It is manifested by an apparently continual state of anestrus. The queen doesn't show any of the usually dramatic signs of proestrus, and in the absence of a breeding tom on the premises, you are never sure what phase of the estrous cycle she is in. Usually, when the time is right, a queen experiencing silent estrus will accept the advances of a mature tom, and will successfully mate with him. The problem is determining the correct time to take her to him.

Vaginal cytology or blood hormone concentration analysis (see page 44) may provide sufficient information to allow successful breeding. Hormone analysis requires laboratory assistance that is usually available through your veterinarian, using commercial biochemical laboratories or veterinary university labs. Repeated blood sampling is necessary for accurate diagnosis of the problem, and although the technique is trustworthy, it's also expensive.

Vaginal cytology analysis can be done by veterinarians in most animal hospitals, but it also requires multiple sampling to be diagnostic. It is less expensive and slightly less accurate than blood hormone analysis, but is a very valuable tool.

One often overlooked cause for unapparent estrus is an actual lack of estrus. Spayed queens are occasionally marketed as breeding animals, and a close examination for an abdominal scar is the first part of any veterinary examination related to silent heat.

Medical histories reveal other causes for unapparent estrus. Queens that have received progesterone products to prevent heat signs may continue in a diestrus state indefinitely. Luteal cysts that continually produce progesterone may be another cause. Certain ovarian tumors and pituitary malfunction are factors in rare cases.

Another tool used to diagnose the causes of silent heats is the laparoscope. Under a short-term general anesthetic, fiber-optic instruments are introduced into the queen's abdomen through a very small incision. The ovaries are observed and changes are recorded repeatedly over a period of several days. The technique is very helpful but expensive. It is usually only available in practices specializing in theriogenology (the study of reproduction), or in university veterinary teaching hospitals. Laparoscopy may also identify other breeding problems such as ovarian inactivity, lack of ovulation after breeding, spontaneous ovulation, and cystic ovaries.

Another tried and true method to solve the mystery of silent heats is to house the problem queen with a proven stud cat. Because queens cycle frequently, the process should take less than a month. It is important to closely observe the attitudes of both tom and queen when they are introduced. If the tom has been used in a colony breeding program, he will quickly accept the fact that she is not in season, and won't press the issue until she is ready, but kenneled breeding toms can be very aggressive when queens are brought to them. Because she may not be in heat, she may resent and reject his courting and mating advances. The possibility of injury exists, and they should be closely observed for at least a few hours before they are left alone.

After the cause for the silent heat is identified, therapy may be initiated. In some cases, simply changing the timing of the breeding program may work. In more complex situations, hormone therapy and artificial insemination may be neces-

sary. Unfortunately, diagnostic tests and hormone therapy are often cost prohibitive, and in those cases, the queen is spayed and placed in a good home or kept as a pet.

Conformation and Maturity

Conformation is a term that refers to the physical description of an animal. It compares the structure, shape, and proportionate dimensions of one animal to other animals of the same species, variety, and breed. In other words, an animal's conformation describes how the physical characteristics of that particular animal conform to the standards set for the breed.

Canines have very plastic genetic characteristics, which accounts for the tremendous variation in appearance among the hundreds of dog breeds. Thus conformation standards for one canine breed differ

Ocicats.

greatly from those of another breed. However, conformation is similar in all purebred domestic felines.

At this time, no one has developed a cat breed with outlandish physical features that interfere with breeding. There is no breed with gigantic forequarters and a skinny pelvis like the English bulldog. No one has produced cats with such short legs and long bodies that they can't breed naturally. It would seem that purebred cat fanciers wish to promote athletic, natural conformation in all breeds. For this reason, feline conformation is rarely the cause of breeding failure.

Female Breeding Failures

Breeding problems are anticipated if a small, young queen in heat is introduced to a large, experienced stud cat. That is not to say that mating won't happen, but it will likely be more traumatic than necessary. A minor size disparity between breeding animals can cause temporary problems, but an experienced tom will adjust his neck grip and body position to accommodate a female with a slightly longer or shorter body or legs than usual.

Before a queen is bred for the first time, her strength and body structure should be carefully evaluated. Physically immature cats shouldn't be bred, regardless of their ages. Some breeds, and certainly some individuals within any breed,

mature slowly. A sure way to evaluate size standards for breeding is to enter the queen in cat shows where she will be critically evaluated. If she fails those tests, perhaps she will fit better into the pet class and should not be part of the genetic pool of a breeding program.

The same rationale applies to breeding toms. If at maturity they are not within the standard size limits and can't pass a judge's scrutiny, castration should be considered.

Breeding Refusal

When a queen in season fails to display the usual mating acceptance, the problem may be nothing more than shyness. Some queens, especially if they are the only cats in their homes, are quite timid when another cat is introduced. To prevent her bashfulness, introduce her to the male several times on a daily basis before the mating time. Leave them together for a short time, then separate them again. Repeated exposure to the tom should relieve her anxiety and breeding should be uneventful when she begins estrus. As stated previously, injury from fighting may result if a tom and queen are put together without chaperones. Don't allow a get-acquainted session to become combative.

Besides shyness, some queens will only mate with certain toms. They may not accept the mates you have chosen, and reject them physically. Although a very aggressive tom may overcome the queen's reluctance, she may actually fight with him and injuries can result. When mate selection refusal is suspected, the best course is to locate another acceptable tom.

Tom refusal to breed is usually associated with foreign breeding environment or youth. When an inexperienced, shy male is transported to the queen's house, his fright may take precedence over his sexual urge and he may be reluctant to breed. If he doesn't display aggressive courting and mating overtures, the female may soon become disenchanted and refuse to cooperate.

When breeding cats, it's best if one of the two knows something about what is going to happen. Cat breeding is therefore easiest if one of the participants has previous breeding experience. A youthful, inexperienced male should be slowly introduced to a queen in the same way described above. A *multiparous* queen (having had previous litters) will usually assist him by calling, coaxing, rubbing, and encouraging him.

Physical Abnormalities

Cats, like other species, are sometimes born with physical, congenital anomalies. Not all birth defects are hereditary, but some are. Breeds developed from limited gene pools are most likely to display hereditary problems. That is one reason why purebred felines are probably more prone to congenital physical anomalies than feral cat populations. When breeding animals

Maine coon kitten.

are selected solely on the basis of coat character, eye color, head shape, or tail length, breeders may inadvertently produce animals with common recessive genetic characteristics. In the process of developing a set of specific features, other less obvious and less desirable features creep into the bloodline. Fortunately, felines in general are not plagued with congenital deformities that affect breeding.

Congenital Deformities

Chest compression, also known by the human anatomical term *pectus excavatum*, is generally considered to be genetically transmitted in cats. It is believed by some to be associated with nutrition of the dam, and it may be a combination of both. It is seen in varying degrees of severity. If you acquire a kitten that you suspect has chest compression, the breeder should be notified and your veterinarian should be consulted immediately for diagnosis and prognosis. The parents of chest compression kittens should be removed from the breeding program because the condition is assumed to be genetically transmitted until proven otherwise.

Patellar (knee cap) displacement is another congenital deformity that has been reported in various breeds. It is assumed to be genetically transmitted as well. The condition is not life threatening, and can usually be surgically repaired, giving a normal life to the affected pet. Affected cats shouldn't be used in a breeding program.

Congenital hip dysplasia has been diagnosed in felines on occasion. More information on hip dysplasia is available in the canine, where it is known to be hereditary. If the same holds true in cats, affected animals should not be used for breeding.

Vaginal deformities, hermaphrodites, and penis deformities are rare in cats. They should be suspected when breeding attempts fail, and veterinary examination should diagnose the specific problems. Congenital problems of those types are not usually correctable, and their possible hereditability should be studied before any corrective therapy is considered.

Conception Failures

When a normal, healthy queen fails to conceive from a normal breeding, it is well to evaluate the tom. Sterility in breeding age toms is not commonly seen, but it does occur. I believe the most common causes for male sterility are genetic or trauma to or infection of the genital organs. In Bengal cat males, the first two or three generations removed from the wild Asian leopard cat are sterile. The rare male calico cats of all breeds are all reported to be sterile. I have heard of male sterility in purebred cats that are the progeny of repeated inbreeding.

Cryptorchidism and Male Failures

Retained testicles (cryptorchidism) is another uncommon condition that results in tom sterility. In my many years of practice I only remember one cat with both testicles retained in its abdomen. More cases of monorchidism were seen, wherein one testicle is retained in the abdomen and the other is normally descended into the scrotum. Monorchid toms will usually be virile and fertile.

Prostatitis

Prostatic diseases are much in the news today. Prostate gland disorders are frequently diagnosed in men, and are also quite common in male dogs. Cats, however, are apparently never afflicted with similar problems. In my years of practice, I never diagnosed feline prostatitis, nor have I heard it discussed in veterinary seminars. Although feline prostate glands are diagrammed and described in anatomy books, I have not found a reference to feline prostatic disease in veterinary texts. The absence of such reference leads me to conclude that the feline prostate either doesn't exist, or that it is not subject to infection or cancer.

Breeding History

Healthy queens are not often problem breeders. When pregnancy doesn't follow normal breeding of a normal, healthy queen to a proven male, the first step toward therapy is to carefully evaluate her breeding history. Her age, frequency of pregnancies, number of kittens per litter, nutritional status, general health, and mates should be considered. Recorded medical and reproductive histories are invaluable when breeding failures occur.

Endocrine Causes

In some cases, the reason for lack of conception may be hormonal. Although it is true that ovulation is stimulated by coitus, the hormone causing ovulation (LH) is produced in proportion to the degree of stimulation afforded by coitus. Individual queens' response to coitus varies from animal to animal. If understimulated, the quantity of LH produced is small, and ovulation may not occur. In other words, the magnitude and duration of the LH production is critical, and it varies depending on coital stimulus.

Ordinarily, ovulation occurs subsequent to breeding, but laboratory studies indicate that spontaneous ovulation is seen in some queens. If

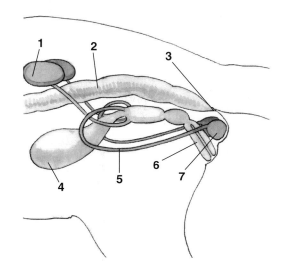

Male genitalia. 1 = Left kidney, 2 = Colon, 3 = Anus, 4 = Urinary bladder, 5 = Left vas deferens, 6 = Retracted penis, 7 = Left testicle.

Reproductive organs of the tom.

the queen ovulates without copulatory stimulus, her proestrus and estrus signs may be abbreviated.

If inadequate LH response or spontaneous ovulation are suspected as potential causes for breeding failure, try leaving the queen with the male constantly from the beginning of the first proestrus signs until she refuses to stand for him. Sometimes repeated breeding stimulation is necessary to achieve the required blood level of LH to cause ovulation.

Queens may fail to conceive for various other reasons, most of which are associated with either disease or nutritional causes. Imprudent inbreeding may result in conception failures, lowered number of kittens born, neonatal weakness and deaths, as well as other reproduction problems.

Litter Size

Research data indicates that about 85 percent of feline ovarian follicles produce ova, and approximately 65 percent of the ova released during ovulation result in kittens. If a cat produces seven follicles, perhaps six ova will be released, resulting in a litter of four kittens. Whether potential embryo losses occur prior to uterine implantation or afterward is undocumented. Many students of the species believe that litter size control is simply an innate feline survival feature. It reduces sibling competition and may be another mechanism that guarantees surviving kittens sufficient nutrition for rapid growth and maturation.

Litter size usually varies from two to five kittens, depending upon the age and parity of the queen. *Parity* (the number of pregnancies experienced by a queen) is an important factor. The first litter is usually small; subsequent litters are larger; then after seven or eight litters, the number of surviving kittens per litter is reduced.

Nutrition is another constant factor that influences litter size and kitten health. It is logical to assume that a queen suffering from marginal or poor nutrition will not produce large litters of strong kittens.

Prebreeding Evaluation

As mentioned previously, breed faults should be recognized and both males and females that do not meet the standards for the breed should be neutered and accepted as pets. Only animals that are fine examples of a breed should join the genetic pool to propagate the breed. In most cases, that means cat show wins under several judges, in competition with a significant number of other cats of the same breed and sex.

Congenital deformities will usually be discovered in the show ring. Even if certain deformities aren't specifically addressed in the breed standard, judges are on the lookout for undesirable congenital conditions. All congenital problems are not necessarily hereditary, but unless proven otherwise, they should eliminate individuals from the breeding pool. There is no excuse for breeding either toms or queens that display undesirable conformation such as undersize, short legs, stumpy tails, splayed feet, or extra toes.

Congenital weakness is another relative condition that should prevent an animal from joining the reproductive pool. If a kitten's development lags behind others in the litter, and if it is frequently ill or demonstrates poor appetite, lethargy, and apathy, it should not be considered brood stock material.

Infectious Diseases

Feline leukemia virus (FeLV) is a major consideration in catteries. (See Infectious Diseases with Available Vaccines, page 132.) Testing and vaccinations can usually identify and prevent the disease. Other systemic diseases that grossly affect breeding include feline panleukopenia, hemobartonellosis, and feline infectious peritonitis. Carrier states exist in several of the feline upper respiratory viral diseases that can affect reproduction as well.

Queens will occasionally contract vaginal infections that limit their breeding potential. Vaginitis is easily diagnosed by a veterinarian, and frequently bacterial cultures are necessary to discover the specific causative organism responsible for the infection.

Breeding Date Selection

By the time your queen has reached breeding age, her estrous cycle should be following a regular pattern and, therefore, choosing a breeding date is simple. Presumably she was thoroughly examined by a veterinarian prior to purchase, but another examination should be scheduled before breeding. Both she and her mate should receive a professional health and soundness examination, preferably by the same veterinarian, about two weeks before the projected breeding.

A stool sample should be taken to the clinic to have her checked for internal parasites at the time of the examination. At the same time, she should be vaccinated for several common feline diseases. Those vaccinations are critically important to protect her health, and to assure that her antibody level is at a peak when the kittens are born.

Examination of the reproductive organs of a queen that has not exhibited breeding problems will be limited. The uterus is sometimes palpable, and the external genitalia is visible, but visual examination of the vagina usually requires heavy sedation and is rarely performed without specific need. Similarly, a tom's testicles are easily examined, but, even in a docile male, penis examination is rarely possible without sedation.

A complete physical examination of both mates is always indicated. The veterinarian will check for signs of contagious diseases, physical deformities, and other problems that might interfere with breeding or pregnancy. Blood tests may be advised, depending on the local incidence of various disease entities.

If your queen is to be shipped or taken to a tom for breeding, as is often the case, be sure the tom's owners have him examined before your queen arrives. A stud cat may contract infections from queens he has served, and those diseases may be passed on to your cat. Insist on seeing a health certificate before finalizing the breeding contract. It is prudent management to speak with the tom's veterinarian about the immediate general health of the tom, even if a health certificate is available.

The veterinarians performing prebreeding examinations should also

A platinum Burmese tom.

have access to health and reproductive histories of the animals. Their vaccination histories, blood test results, fecal exam results, past diseases, and treatments employed should be considered. Previous breeding dates, numbers and frequency of litters produced, and mortality of kittens born to both parents are also important factors to include in breeding soundness evaluations.

The economics of prebreeding examinations are often questioned by novice cat breeders. I think you will find that the fees charged are modest compared to the cost of disease therapy or reproductive function loss. Vaccinations are invaluable, and their timing is equally important. Protective immunity only results when the vaccine is administered to healthy cats.

Chapter 5
Breeding Process

Choose the mating time carefully. Remember that you must be ready to care for your queen during pregnancy, assist in delivery if necessary, properly care for the kittens, and locate suitable homes for them. Look ahead nine weeks and be sure your calendar is free at the time queening will take place. Six to eight weeks after delivery you will face weaning chores, advertising for new homes, and some kitten training duties. Don't schedule a breeding date in the middle of October if you expect a houseful of Christmas guests.

Introducing the Mates

If an experienced tom is being used, the place of breeding is somewhat irrelevant. If it is the first mating for your queen, and if the male's owner agrees, you may decide to transport the tom to the queen. He is more likely to be aggressive, and she will be less shy in familiar surroundings. You should be aware that owners of breeding toms may not

turn their valuable stud cats over to you without restrictions. Remember also that all breeding toms come equipped with foul smelling spraying habits with which you must contend if you bring one into your home.

In most cases, the queen should be taken to the tom, for several reasons. Breeding toms require special facilities that owners of queens may not be able to provide. Some toms are reluctant to breed in strange surroundings, but queens in proestrus

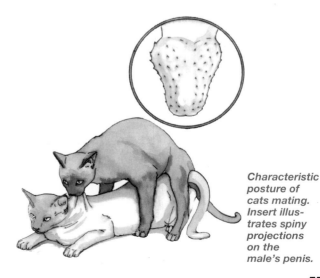

Characteristic posture of cats mating. Insert illustrates spiny projections on the male's penis.

back arched downward, and tail to the side. After those initial overtures have been played for an hour, open his kennel and take an inconspicuous seat from which to observe.

Ordinarily, if the queen is in estrus, she will begin calling, flirting, and rubbing against him, acting very seductive. He, in turn, will continue the low throaty moaning, and usually will pace about, occasionally taking a light grip on her neck with his teeth.

If the queen tries to escape from him, hides, seeks refuge on your lap, or otherwise acts unwilling to allow the male to mount her, it's possible that she is not yet ready for actual mating. If he continually grasps her by the neck and tries to mount against her will, it's best to separate them for a day. If the tom is not pressing the issue and is content to wait for her, it is a common and logical practice to leave them together, alone in the room. In a controlled breeding program, it is prudent to leave the pair together, separated from other animals and humans, for an entire day or two. The most productive time of mating is the second to the fifth day of her visible heat signs.

If allowed, cats will mate several times a day, and the probability of conception increases with repeated matings. On occasion, a male may be overly aggressive, and a queen may be injured if they are left together unmonitored for extended periods. In those cases, you should kennel one of the pair, preferably the male, except during the actual matings.

or estrus usually adapt more quickly to new facilities. Most queens in season are notably aggressive wherever they are.

Cats should always be transported in a well-constructed carrier. Whether shipping her across the country or taking her to a neighbor's cattery, a strong fiberglass carrier is a must.

Once she arrives at the breeding location, leave her in the carrier in a room where the tom is kept. A gentle, formal introduction of the bride and groom is advisable. To accomplish that, leave the male in his kennel and allow the queen to approach him, beginning the mating prelude through the bars of the kennel. The queen will first investigate the new surroundings, and gradually she will approach the tom's kennel to sniff noses and talk to him. Soon she will begin to show signs of the breeding stance; that is, rubbing her face on the floor with her hind end elevated,

The Mating Ritual

The mating ritual of cats doesn't require human intervention. Occasionally, the mating will take place as soon as you open the male's cage. Sometimes, however, a measure of feline decorum demands privacy in order for the connubial functions to evolve. In case the pair do not approach each other in your presence, leave the room, and watch them through a window or a cracked door.

If the floor of the breeding area is tiled or slick, provide a big throw rug for the lovers. A surface providing good traction is very desirable to accomplish the mating ritual with the least difficulty.

As is the case with many other team projects, more predictable results are achieved when the male or female, or both, are experienced in the mating game. A young tom that has not yet sired a litter will probably perform adequately with your virgin queen, but an experienced tom would be preferable.

Don't be surprised at the moaning, yowling, and other cries that emanate from the tom and queen. Cats are usually quite vocal during mating. The male will usually court his mate with low guttural sounds for a few minutes, then he will grasp the female's dorsal neck skin in his teeth. That act, an essential part of successful mating, often precipitates some sounds of anguish from the queen. Inexperienced males may be unable to properly position

Tom with neck grasp.

their bodies because of an incorrect neck grasp.

The tom will quickly mount the queen from the side, stepping on her hind leg while maintaining his hold on the skin of her neck. In response to his rough but amorous advances, the female holds her tail to one side and points her posterior upward. In a few seconds, as he finalizes his role in the reproductive act, the female will emit a reverberating howl that is hard to miss if you are in the same neighborhood.

As painful as it all sounds, the couple is usually anxious to repeat the performance in two or three hours. After a few matings have been observed, mark your calendar. In 63 days kittens should arrive.

Aftercare of the Queen

You can expect the female to continue to show mild signs of heat for a few days after mating, but her appetite and personality should return to normal within a day or two

after the stress of estrus and breeding is over.

After the last mating, dampen the hair of the back of the queen's neck with alcohol and examine the skin carefully. There are often a few tooth marks that are superficial and rarely cause any problems. They should be left alone to scab and heal. Puncture wounds that extend through the skin are rarely the result of mating, but if any penetrations are noted, they should be examined and treated by your veterinarian.

Artificial Insemination (A.I.)

Only in rare instances is artificial insemination (A.I.) a viable option to natural breeding. When it is deemed necessary, A.I. should be left in the hands of experienced theriogenologists or veterinarians who have studied the process and who are properly equipped to perform the procedure. The technique is well

defined, and when it becomes more familiar to practicing veterinarians, it may save breeders money spent in shipping valuable queens across the country to desirable males.

If popularized, A.I. should have significant use in cases of rare breeds where the gene pool is very limited. It may also extend the breeding life of an exceptional tom beyond his own lifetime. It could provide breeding access to toms in another country without the usual importation of health regulations.

Semen can be collected from male cats by either of two techniques: artificial vaginas or electroejaculation. Males in an A.I. program using artificial vagina collection techniques require extensive training, and a teaser queen is used to arouse them to perform. Electroejaculation is accomplished with the tom under light anesthesia. In either case, the semen collected may be frozen for shipping or storing for future use, or it may be used fresh. In either case, evaluation of the sperm cells, including their numbers, motility, and conformation should precede their insemination into the queen.

To assure ovulation, queens that are bred by A.I. require artificial vaginal stimulation following insemination. Some practitioners prefer to stimulate ovulation with a hormone injection; others massage the vaginal vault with a sterile, smooth plastic probe. In either case, A.I. has a reasonable success rate and may be employed to a greater extent in the future.

Chapter 6
Pregnancy

Duration

The average length of pregnancy in domestic cats is 63 days. The published gestation period for all cats ranges from 59 to 65 days. Yet, normal pregnant queens have been reported to carry a normal litter to the 65th, 68th, or 70th day of gestation. When your veterinarian finds no problems in spite of the gestation time, and, if the queen continues to eat normally, act normally, and no foul vaginal discharge is noted, she will very likely deliver her kittens by her own calendar, regardless of charts and predictions.

Embryonic Activity

A male's sperm cell contains only half the number of chromosomes of a normal body cell (it is a *haploid* cell). Likewise, an ovum is also haploid. These germ cells are technically known as male and female *haploid gametes*. When they unite, the resulting cell is called a *zygote*, which is the first cell of a new kitten. The zygote is *diploid*, that is it contains twice the number of chromosomes found in either the sperm or ovum. Its chromosome number is the same as the body (somatic) cells of each parent. All body cells are termed diploid.

The uniting of sperm cells with ova (fertilization), takes place in the oviducts. The zygotes rapidly divide into two cells that divide into four, eight, and so on. These fast-growing embryos travel quickly through the oviducts and into the horns of the queen's uterus (see illustration, page 40). The lining of the uterine horns is specially designed tissue that invites implantation of the embryonic

Siamese exhibits gross changes in phenotype.

61

tissues. The embryos become attached to the uterine walls in a rather happenstance pattern.

When performing cesarean sections, I have found all fetuses in one horn on occasion, but usually they are split more or less half in one horn and half in the other. Rarely are placentas attached in the body of the uterus.

As soon as embryos have found their implantation sites, a complexity of tissues surround them. Growing from embryonic sources, the placenta is formed. It is made up of sacs and vessels that support embryonic life. Placental sacs contain fluids that cushion the embryos from one another and from external trauma. The umbilical cord contains blood vessels that supply nutrition to the new life. It is interesting to note that although the dam's blood courses through the fetal vessels, there is no direct linkage between them. Rather, the maternal blood components are absorbed or diffused through the thin, vascular membranous barrier between the uterus and placenta. The process of fluid and nutrient exchange between the dam and the fetus is called *transplacental transfer*.

Some elements easily cross the placental barrier; others do not. For instance, antibodies, which are protein molecules, do not appreciably cross that barrier, and thus kittens receive practically none of their mother's immunity before they are born. Some pathogens, such as the distemper (panleukopenia) virus, cross the barrier

with ease, and kittens may be aborted or born with infections caused by those pathogens.

Each embryo forms its own placental attachment, making each one independent of its siblings from the beginning of life. That accounts for the occasional partial abortion, or resorption of embryos. It is possible for a single fetus to die, remain in the uterus and undergo mummification, and yet not disturb the normal, healthy growth and delivery of other fetuses in the same uterine horn.

The terms embryo and fetus are used here almost interchangeably because there is no clearly established rule for their use. Generally, the term embryo is used while the new life is organizing, before definitive organs and systems are grossly identifiable. I try to use *embryo* in connection with the first three weeks of life. Likewise, I reserve *fetus* for the stage of life after organ differentiation is present, during the last six weeks of gestation.

I have often been asked about fetal intestinal and urinary activity. Unborn kittens receive all their nutrition from their dams through their umbilical cords, and waste products are eliminated by a reversal of the process. Even though fetuses consume nothing orally, they do produce both urine and feces. The fetal urine is handled by the placental structure, but the semisolid feces is stored in the kitten's bowel until birth. It is a dark, greenish black, sticky material called *meconium* that is usually expelled soon after birth.

Meconium is sometimes seen at the time of uncomplicated queening, but normally the dam's licking and massaging stimulates its expulsion, and she consumes it immediately. Meconium is usually quite apparent when kittens are delivered by cesarean section.

Pregnancy Determination

To date, there is no accepted blood or urine test to reliably determine feline pregnancy. X rays are not usually a viable option, due to the possibility of radiation damage to the fetuses. Ultrasound imaging is sometimes used, but it too is not totally danger-free. Ordinarily, the sensitive hands of an experienced veterinarian can palpate the uterus and diagnose feline pregnancies between 15 and 20 days of gestation. At that time, the embryos are firm, spherical structures about the size of small marbles. Abdominal palpation should not be attempted by someone who is inexperienced in proper technique.

At about four weeks of gestation, queens will display some abdominal enlargement, and usually their nipples will begin to appear more prominent. As parturition approaches, queens will often pluck out patches of abdominal hair surrounding their nipples. The pregnant queen's general condition should remain constant throughout the 63 days of gestation. A dry, lackluster

Gentle palpation will reveal fetal activity during the final stages of pregnancy.

coat, excessive hair loss, and weight loss is not normal! The appetite should gradually increase, and strenuous activities and play time should decrease as the pregnancy progresses.

Hormonal Changes

Little has been published regarding feline hormonal levels during pregnancy. Endocrine profiles done during the estrus and diestrus phases of the feline's estrous cycle are apparently not very accurate indicators of a queen's reproductive status. The various hormone levels seem to change little from estrus to implantation. Progesterone levels increase rather rapidly after about 45 days of gestation to help maintain pregnancy.

At the time your queen is bred, note the expected date of delivery on your calendar as a reference point, but don't get terribly excited if the kittens arrive a few days on either side of the predicted date. Interestingly, cats with limited exercise often display longer gestation periods than those that remain playful and active throughout pregnancy.

Danger Signs

If the expectant queen stops eating, has an elevated temperature, becomes depressed, or licks excessively at her genitalia during pregnancy, she and her kittens may be in trouble and require medical or surgical intervention. Any significant vaginal discharge prior to queening should tell you that something is wrong. Take the cat's temperature and call the veterinarian.

Scottish fold cat.

Embryonic or Fetal Resorption

A phenomenon commonly encountered in dogs and cats is a spontaneous resorption of fetuses. There are many theories about the cause of resorption; none that fit all cases. There are no outward symptoms to alert owners that resorption is taking place. The queen doesn't show signs of illness and there is no bloody or foul vaginal discharge. For some reason, the embryos or fetuses are gradually absorbed by the queen and the pregnancy is terminated. In other instances, only one or two are resorbed, and the remaining kittens are carried to normal term and born alive and healthy.

More than once I have detected five or six distinct fetal structures in a queen's uterus at 18 days of gestation. A week later, the count was the same and they were even more palpable. When she delivered a healthy litter of three kittens, my ego and credibility suffered greatly. Then I got wise and stopped predicting numbers, or if an owner pressed me for that information, I carefully explained fetal resorption.

Abortion

Abortion is relatively common in cats. It may involve the loss of all fetuses or only a portion of them, and may occur at any stage of gestation. It is manifested by discernible embryos or fetuses being delivered prematurely. Survey reports indicate that about 2 percent of all feline pregnancies end in abortion, and only about a fifth of the aborted fetuses had anatomical deformities. Most abortions go unrecorded, due to the queens' propensity to consume the aborted tissue.

Other Prenatal Kitten Losses

Besides abortion and resorption, fetuses sometimes die, are mummified, and retained in the queen's uterus. Extra-uterine mummified fetuses are occasionally found also. They result from the fertilization of an ovum that somehow escapes from the oviducts, lives, and grows outside the uterus. When its life can no longer be supported by its extra-uterine attachment, it dies and mummifies. Examination by abdominal palpation or x-ray often identifies these structures as mummies, but I have surgically removed one that I believed to be a tumor prior to surgical exploration.

Stillborn kittens comprise over one third of all preweaning kitten losses. Of those, most are found to have very low birth weights.

Causes for Prenatal Deaths

A great deal of research has been done to identify causes of fetal losses, and those investigations continue to uncover various genetic information. Chromosome abnormalities have been described by many authors, but in most cases, fetal losses are attributed to infectious agents.

Abortions, stillbirths, and neonatal deaths are commonly found associated with feline panleukopenia (distemper) virus exposure. The feline leukemia virus (FeLV) has been incriminated with epidemic levels of abortion in large catteries, and feline viral rhinotracheitis (FVR or herpes virus) has also been associated with prenatal fetal losses.

The feline infectious peritonitis (FIP) virus has been associated with sterility, abortion, stillbirth, and neonatal deaths. Published information on this virus has been accumulated from catteries where breeding females have positive blood titers for FIP. That means there is a potential margin for error in the reports, because the antibody test is not specific.

Other causes for abortion include *Salmonella* bacteria, and the protozoan organism causing toxoplasmosis. Trauma during pregnancy may cause placental detachment and abortion. Certain drugs, including aspirin, steroids, some sulfas, and a few antibiotics, have been identified as known causes for abortion and fetal resorption.

Diet and Exercise Changes

A queen's caloric demands increase dramatically at about the second week of pregnancy. Between the tenth day and the fifty-sixth day, the daily caloric intake will increase by at least 70 percent. The body weight will be increased by 25 percent by the fourth week of gestation. This early weight gain is probably related to rapid embryonic growth and increased fat storage in the queen that will supply calories needed for milk production.

Isn't it interesting that a cat's reproductive metabolism is synchronized to take advantage of its historic hunting ability? Early in pregnancy, queens remain strong and active, and that is when their caloric demands are highest. Later, as they become clumsy, heavy, and less active, their nutritional demands decrease. The scenario is nearly opposite to that seen in dogs.

Another rather unique aspect of feline pregnancy is their retention of weight after parturition. When pregnancy is terminated in dogs, the bitch loses virtually all the weight she gained during gestation. Not so the feline! Normal queens will retain some of their weight gain, and are typically 20 percent heavier after queening than before they were bred. Those features probably contribute to the cat's reputation as a good mother or reproductive expert.

The previously discussed reproductive nutrition recommendations (see Feeding Brood Stock, page 23) apply to pregnancy diets with one additional comment. If possible, weigh your queen and record her weight weekly from the time she is bred throughout gestation and lactation. If her gains do not approximate those expected, a veterinary consultation is indicated. An obscure parasite infestation or metabolic problem might be discovered and treated before serious effects are realized.

In nearly every case, if your pregnant queen is fed with free access to a premium quality dry cat food, there is no reason to change or to add supplements to her diet. If supplements are used, they must be totally balanced. For instance, premium canned food may be offered twice daily in addition to the dry product. If both foods carry the AAFCO label, stating that they supply appropriate nutrition for the entire feline life cycle, as determined by AAFCO feeding trials, they should meet the pregnant cat's needs. They will contain the correct amounts and ratios of protein, fat, carbohydrates, minerals, and vitamins. Recommended products are those that contain at least 30 percent protein and 30 percent fat (metabolizable energy). That translates to labels stating 30 percent protein and 14 percent fat in dry foods, and 8½ percent protein and 4 percent fat for canned cat food. Gestation diet ingredients should be primarily of animal origin.

Labels that claim only to meet NRC recommendations for all stages of the life cycle are not necessarily adequate for pregnancy and lactation, and I caution you not to rely on them. I also caution you not to supplement balanced diets with additional meat, milk, cheese, or eggs.

Supplements and Homemade Diets

Vitamin and mineral supplements may also be contraindicated and should be added to gestation diets only upon the advice of a veterinarian. Some of the fat-soluble vitamins are toxic to cats in excess quantities, and certain minerals may also cause problems in both queens and their kittens.

Homemade diets are also dangerous in my opinion. Unless you have the equipment and ability to analyze all ingredients, you shouldn't try to compete with cat food manufacturers. Many so-called natural diets do not take into consideration the rather unique amino acid requirements of cats. If you have the facilities, time, equipment, and other resources to formulate diets, and you can prove your work through controlled feeding trials, go for it. For guidance and information on homemade diets, refer to the previously mentioned book, *Nutrient Requirements of Cats* (see page 22), from the NRC.

Generic Cat Foods

In my experience, most generic and house brands of cat foods do not meet the criteria for gestation and lactation diets. Keep in mind that cats have specific reproductive requirements for certain amino acids including arginine and taurine, as well as retinol, niacin, and arachidonic acid. Successful cat breeding demands a sound nutritional basis. Don't economize on cat food quality.

Appetite and Weight Gain

By 10 to 14 days into pregnancy, your queen's appetite will begin to gradually increase until shortly before parturition. Her appetite will often decrease for a few days at about 21 days of gestation. At that time her weight gain will stop until the appetite returns, within a week. Often owners become alarmed by that normal appetite reduction and begin to change food. Your queen's diet should not be adjusted when that dip in her appetite is observed. It is a normal, physiological pattern in all pregnant queens. Her appetite will again wane during the last day or two of gestation.

During gestation, her food intake will be at least 25 percent higher than her maintenance level. A queen normally weighing 7½ pounds (3.4 kg) will probably weigh over 11 pounds (4.9 kg) at delivery time. The increased weight is due to growing fetuses, placental tissues, fluids, and developing mammary glands.

Dip their muzzles in the gravy.

She should continue to be active and playful for at least five or six of her nine weeks of gestation. The last two or three weeks, as her abdomen becomes pendulous and turgid, her physical activities will decrease.

Attitude Changes

As the time for parturition nears, you can expect your outgoing, affectionate queen to become more reclusive. She will seek out a secluded place and spend more time away from your family than usual. She may also become more possessive of that place of refuge. During the last two weeks of gestation, when she lies on her side, you can observe the fetuses changing positions. It is OK to gently lay your palm on her abdomen to feel the activity of the kittens, but don't invite strangers, especially children, to do so. An expectant queen may be more loving than usual toward her favorite people, and at the same time she may resent the attentions of children, pets, and strangers.

Maternity Ward

In normal pregnancies, as the expectant queen becomes more reclusive, you should provide her a room or a large wire kennel that is off-limits to children and other pets. That maternity room might be a small bathroom or an unused bedroom. It should be light, and kept at the usual household temperature. Furnish the room or large cage with her litter pan, food, water, and a nesting box. During the last week of pregnancy, she should be confined to her maternity room except when with the family. If you fail to heed this advice, you can expect to find a litter of kittens on your bed pillow when you return from an evening out.

Nesting Box

The nesting box need be nothing more elaborate than a cave fashioned from an enclosed cardboard carton with an opening in one end. The size of her box should be large enough to allow the expectant mother to stretch out in any direction. It must later accommodate the queen and her brood of four or five kittens for a week. The box should be small enough to confine the infant kittens within reach of their mother. A box with a top, which is more or less 2 feet (0.6 m) square,

If given the opportunity, queens may deliver their broods in undesirable places.

and 1 foot (0.3 m) tall, with a 6 inch (15.2 cm) diameter hole cut in one end about 3 inches (7.6 cm) from the floor is adequate (see illustration).

Bedding

Pillows, loose towels, or blankets should not be used in the nest box until the kittens are at least two weeks old. Prior to that time, avoid all bedding material that a newborn kitten can crawl under, thus separating itself from its mother and siblings. The best floor surface for a nest is soft and flat, extending from wall to wall in the box. A covered piece of clean, short-nap carpet cut to fit the bottom of the box is ideal. Stretch a layer or two of fabric, such as a towel, over the carpet and tuck it tightly beneath the carpet around the edges. Avoid nesting materials that are shaggy or those with a nap that might produce bits of fuzz that can be a source of trouble for the kittens. Materials with loops or fringes that may trap kittens' feet should never be used as bedding. Keep in mind that queening is messy, and floor coverings must be changed and washed frequently.

Drugs During Pregnancy

Avoid administration of all drugs during your cat's pregnancy if possible. Carefully consider the need for flea and tick repellents, as well as other insecticide-containing products that you might use on or around your

An inexpensive maternity ward and kitten nursey.

pet. Cats are quite sensitive to many topical parasite control products, and during pregnancy, they become doubly dangerous. Consult with your veterinarian before you place a flea collar on your queen or spray your carpets for fleas or ticks.

Aspirin is always contraindicated in cats, but it is even more dangerous to administer to pregnant queens. Certain antibiotics also cross the placental barrier and may cause fetal death or deformities. A good rule to follow is to avoid giving pregnant queens anything except food and water. If she is ill or injured, and any drugs are prescribed by your veterinarian, be sure you discuss the possible side effects of the products to be used.

Anesthetics may also be harmful to unborn kittens, but sometimes they are unavoidable. Generally, anesthetic agents will be chosen that do not cause fetal problems, providing that the veterinarian knows the queen is pregnant. I have safely anesthetized many pregnant queens for treatment of fractures, wounds, or other emergencies. It is important to tell your veterinarian when the queen was bred before anesthesia is begun.

Elective Pregnancy Termination

There are many reasons to arbitrarily terminate a pregnancy. Maybe your carefully protected purebred queen that had been yowling for a couple of days, escaped from the house, was gone for a day, and returned with a smile on her face. You didn't suspect she had been bred until she began to eat excessively and gain weight.

Perhaps your registered show cat was purposefully mated to a tom that later proved to be a close relative or to have some very undesirable characteristic. Maybe he was misrepresented at the time of breeding, and his problem only surfaced when you later studied his pedigree or health records.

Cats that range outdoors often reach sexual maturity without their owners' knowledge. Queens with that lifestyle will almost surely be bred on their first heat.

Perhaps you adopted your pet from a shelter, and discovered a few weeks later that she was in a family way.

An unexpected change in your own housing, living arrangement, or lifestyle may make it impossible to properly accommodate or care for a litter of kittens. These reasons for pregnancy termination are a few that I have encountered; I'm sure there are many more.

Pregnancy termination can be accomplished in a variety of ways; none however, without some danger. If the queen is less than two weeks pregnant, estrogenic hormones can be administered to interrupt embryo implantation and development. There is, however, a serious side effect to the use of those hormones. They will prolong or artificially induce heat, with all its undesirable caterwauling and other signs. Long-term side effects may possibly be dangerous to the health or life of the queen. Repeated dosages of estrogens have been incriminated as causes of pyometra, a serious condition (see page 72). Estrogen administration may also interfere with future estrous cycles, creating breeding problems in the queen. I can't recommend the use of estrogen to terminate pregnancy except as a last resort.

After 40 days of gestation, abortion may be accomplished by use of prostaglandins, which are another class of hormones. They also may produce undesirable side effects, and should be used with discretion, and only by experienced veterinarians.

Surgical termination of feline pregnancies is probably the most reliable and safest procedure. Spaying pregnant queens presents little danger when performed by experienced veterinary surgeons. The only negative aspect of the procedure is the irreversible loss of fertility of the queens. In an ovariohysterectomy (spay) operation, both ovaries and the uterus are removed. The reproductive life of the queen is ended.

A decision to electively terminate your queen's pregnancy should be made only after consultation with a veterinarian who is familiar with every technique currently available. If future kittens are not important, and your major concern is the life and health of your pet, you should carefully consider the surgical option.

False Pregnancy (Pseudocyesis)

When queens are bred but do not conceive, they may display all the typical signs of pregnancy, including weight gain. This condition is not common when natural breeding occurs, except in the rare cases of tomcat sterility. Lack of conception and false pregnancy has been documented in certain females that are bred only once during their standing heat period. Those individuals apparently require repeated copulation to stimulate LH levels sufficient to cause ovulation.

In my experience, pseudocyesis is most often the result of human attempts to stop the noisy, irritating estrus period by artificially simulating coitus.

As indicated in the previous discussion of induced ovulation, the queen ovulates and conceives only following copulation. Occasionally,

veterinarians (and sometimes breeders) attempt to interrupt estrus by inserting a warm, pliable, lubricated, smooth instrument into the queen's vagina, and rubbing it about. The vaginal tickling procedure is intended to stimulate LH production by fooling the pituitary gland into thinking the queen has been bred. When it works, the queen ovulates and the ensuing diestrus phase of her estrous cycle (which is shorter than if she is actually bred), gives the owner a few weeks of relief from her frequent heat periods.

The procedure is not foolproof and can be dangerous when attempted by amateurs. Please do not attempt it at home. Consult with your veterinarian, and if you agree to try it, let the professional perform the procedure. When the anatomy of the genital tract is well known, and care is taken to avoid damage to the fragile vaginal tissues, there is little physical danger to the queen. Unfortunately, the cat's reproductive system sometimes reacts to the simulated breeding by producing all the typical signs of pregnancy. Her attitude may change, mimicking normal gestation, and she may display nesting and labor signs, mammary gland development, and milk production. Only the lack of kittens will convince her that she is not a mother.

False pregnancies should not be cause for worry. They usually terminate in nine weeks or less, and the following estrous cycles will be normal. If repeated false pregnancies follow normal matings, you

should reevaluate your breeding program. The tom's mating performance, his kitten production with other queens, the number of times your queen is mated, and the time of estrus during which she is mated should be considered.

Pyometra

By strict definition, *pyometra* is a disease entity typically involving a uterine bacterial infection. It occurs during diestrus, which is the pregnancy phase of a queen's life, and it mimics normal pregnancy, at least for a little while. It begins shortly after the estrus period. The female gradually becomes heavier, her abdomen enlarges, and she becomes lethargic. In the early phase of the disease, her tempera-

ture is not significantly elevated, and there is no vaginal discharge.

Pyometra is generally believed to be the result of hormone disorders during diestrus. Exaggerated progesterone levels during that reproductive phase influence the *endometrium* (lining of the uterus) to grow, and soften. Glands in the endometrium secrete fluids and the uterine tissues are very vascular as they prepare to receive and furnish support and sustenance for embryos. The glandular fluid provides an excellent medium for bacterial growth, and the growing, vascular tissues are highly susceptible to infection. Bacteria that may be normal residents in the vagina migrate into the uterus while the cervix is dilated during estrus. After bacterial contamination of the uterus, the cervix closes, trapping the infection within the organ. The results of that scenario may be a uterine infection that is devastating, and sometimes even fatal.

The key to pyometra is the hormone progesterone, which is produced naturally from the corpora lutea after ovulation. Because cats only produce corpora lutea after being bred, natural progesterone production normally occurs in pregnant females. That hormone is necessary for embryonic and fetal development.

Many, if not all, cases of pyometra in cats are associated with *artificial* progesterone administration. Extraneous progesterone products may be administered to cats for several reasons. They are sometimes used as fertility controls to prevent heat cycles. Occasionally they are used to treat skin disorders, and I have also known of their use to treat behavioral problems. Regardless of the reason for their use, they can produce serious consequences when given to intact queens.

Estrogens are also commonly incriminated as causes for pyometra. They may be administered to queens that were inadvertently bred, as mismating injections. Sometimes they are used to artificially induce heat in noncycling queens. Estro-

gens increase uterine stimulation by progesterones, and thereby may precipitate pyometra.

As pyometra slowly develops and copious endometrial glandular secretions fill the uterus, bacterial reproduction is overwhelming. Finally, the queen stops eating and becomes extremely lethargic. In its final full-blown form, pyometra is presented to the veterinarian as a surgical emergency. The patient's uterus is distended with perhaps a quart of pus. She is toxic from the absorption of bacterial wastes. She is usually dehydrated, anemic, hypothermic, and on the verge of death.

It is the opinion of many veterinarians, the author included, that the only acceptable treatment for pyometra is an immediate ovariohysterectomy. There is no time for antibiotic therapy, uterine drainage, and other potential treatments. Supportive procedures such as temperature stabilization, dehydration correction, blood transfusions, and antibiotic therapy are frequently employed concurrently with surgery.

Pyometra occurs less frequently in cats than in dogs, but it is just as life threatening when diagnosed. Watch for the signs, especially if estrogen or progesterone products are used on your queen.

Chapter 7
Parturition (Queening)

Too Much Help

A queen in good health rarely requires human assistance with parturition. If you are fortunate enough to witness the birth of kittens, you will be amazed at the instinctive knowledge and abilities that a feline mother possesses. Unnecessary human intervention in a normal kitten delivery may cause several problems. Those difficulties can be avoided if you simply allow the mother to do that which she is capable of and willing to do. Cats are very independent when giving birth, and midwifery is not usually appreciated. In most instances, the breeder should allow the mother to take care of every aspect of parturition providing the delivery progresses in a productive manner. The pace or speed of delivery is irrelevant if she is producing live kittens and cleaning them, and if none appears to be having difficulty breathing.

If you unnecessarily interfere or intervene in a normal parturition process, you must be ready to accept the consequences. I have known queens that received too much help in the delivery of their kittens. Their response was to abandon the litter. When they were prevented from cleaning, licking, and massaging the newborn, they lost interest in them. When they didn't have the opportunity to sever the umbilical cord and eat the placenta, they chose to ignore the kittens. That is another trait that is less pronounced in felines than in canines, but it can occur.

If your queen has difficulty queening, be ready to assist; but if she is handling it on her own, sit back and enjoy the spectacle.

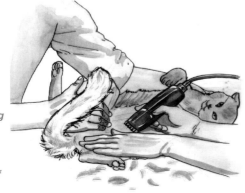

Clip the long hair from belly and perineum during the last week of gestation.

Preparing for Queening

The need for a nesting box and a clean, quiet maternity room has been discussed (see Maternity Ward, page 68). In addition to those preparations, I suggest that you have a few supplies on hand in case delivery assistance is required.

Equipment and Supply List

This equipment will probably never be needed or used, but if you wish to be totally prepared for all eventualities, these items should be made ready:

- 2 pairs of inexpensive hemostat forceps, obtainable from surplus stores, pet supply stores, or swap meets
- a pair of blunt-tipped surgical scissors, available from the same sources.
- several clean, dry wash cloths that are expendable
- 2- or 3-ml hypodermic syringe without a needle
- a small vial of organic, povidone iodine solution, available in drugstores
- a small, shallow pan with a cover, to be used to sterilize the syringe, scissors, and forceps
- several sterile cotton swabs
- a roll of dental floss

A day or two prior to the expected delivery, place the scissors, forceps, and dismantled

syringe in the pan, add sufficient distilled water to cover the instruments, and boil them for 15 minutes. Pour the water off before the pan cools, and leave the dry instruments in the covered pan. Using bottled distilled water will prevent mineral deposits from forming on the instruments during boiling.

Place 1 ounce of the povidone iodine solution in a small, wide-topped vessel the size of a baby food jar or a shot glass.

The use of these items will be explained as you progress into the discussion of kitten delivery, when physical assistance may become necessary (see Chapter 8).

The maternity ward should be a quiet, secluded place.

Predicting Queening Time

There is no perfect way to predict delivery time. Unless the queen has alerted you to her immediate plans, you may open the maternity room door some morning and discover a beautiful litter of kittens contentedly nursing or squirming about the nest. If she decides to apprise you of her queening plans, the early signs of impending labor vary according to the individual cat.

Signs of Labor

If you wish to try to pinpoint the time of labor onset, there are some signs that will help. A 2- or 3-degree drop in her body temperature is a fairly accurate way to predict parturition. A day or two before parturition is expected, begin taking your queen's rectal temperature every eight hours. When the body temperature drops from the normal of 101.5°F (38.5°) to 98°F or 99°F (37°C), active labor should begin within eight to twelve hours.

The earliest outward signs of impending labor to watch for are reduced appetite, restlessness, abnormal breathing, pacing, and frequent trips to her nest. If she stays in her bed, licks at her genitalia persistently, changes her position frequently, and seems uncomfortable, early labor has probably begun.

Stage I Labor

The first stage of labor involves uterine contractions, causing the fetuses to change position and begin to shift toward the body of the uterus. During this period, the kittens remain within their individual placental sacs that are still attached to the lining of the uterine horns.

A clear, mucoid, odorless vaginal discharge is usually apparent at that time. When seen, the discharge will resemble raw egg white. It is stringy and clear, perhaps tinged slightly yellow. It acted as a plug in the cervix during pregnancy, sealing the uterus away from the vaginal vault. As active labor begins, the cervix dilates to open the birth canal, and the seal is extruded into the vagina. It may be noticed sticking to the queen's tail hair or flanks. Delivery may begin within minutes or a few hours after that discharge is observed.

If a green, black, brown, bloody, or foul-smelling discharge is seen before the arrival of the first kitten, call your veterinarian. A greenish black discharge is the result of sepa-

We finished the bread, now where's the milk?

ration of placental attachments to the lining of the uterus. When a placenta detaches, a kitten should be born within minutes. Following the first birth, greenish fluid is routinely seen, and is considered normal. Foul yellow discharges may be related to bacterial infections or decomposing dead kittens.

Some nonclotting, bloody fluid accompanies all births. It is a combination of amniotic fluid from the placenta, blood from the umbilical cord, and other natural fluids.

It is common for a queen to show preliminary signs of labor, then appear normal for a few hours, after which productive labor begins.

Cats experiencing uterine contractions often have difficulty finding a comfortable position. They lie down, stand, turn around, and lie down on the other side. They rarely make cries of discomfort, but when touched by their human friends, purring is often heard.

The duration of Stage I labor varies from queen to queen. Indeed, it may not be observed at all. I have known queens that were walking about the house, even taking a snack of food, then producing their first kittens a few minutes later. Others display pronounced early labor signs over a period of several hours. That is especially true of purebred, pampered animals and those that are the products of linebreeding or inbreeding.

It is important to be aware of early signs of delivery, but don't place a great deal of significance on time elements. Normal progress in the

Though it is rarely necessary to intervene, have supplies ready to assist delivery.

delivery is much more important than how long each phase requires.

Stage II Labor

Second stage labor signs are fairly obvious to observant breeders. The queen will usually lie on her side, and abdominal muscle contractions progress from mild to very strong. This stage might be termed the productive or delivery phase of labor. It relates to the physical and physiological changes that take place when a queen's involuntary uterine muscular contractions are coordinated with her voluntary abdominal muscular contractions. It results in the production of kittens.

Each kitten is normally born in one fluid motion, propelled from the queen's womb by uterine and abdominal muscle contractions. Sometimes the birth process may be observed to occur in several stages. The queen's body is held slightly curved, and often she holds one hind leg raised in the air. It will be obvious by her body position and movements that the queen is apply-

ing abdominal pressure, and some will grunt and strain as they do so.

Within a few minutes, some fluid will escape from the birth canal, followed by a small bubble of thin, balloonlike opaque tissue that is squeezed through the vagina. The bubble is filled with fluid, and as the queen applies more pressure, a pair

A queen cleaning and sorting her newborn kittens.

of tiny feet and a muzzle will become visible in the fluid, within the bubble. Some fluids will be bloodstained; others will appear a greenish color. Copious hemorrhage at this time is not normal, and is cause for alarm. If it is seen, contact your veterinarian immediately.

As a kitten's head emerges from the birth canal, the mother may turn and grasp her newborn, tearing the amniotic membranes from its head. She may grasp the kitten's head and pull on it to assist its entry into the world. In other cases, the abdominal pressure alone will cause the entire kitten to be expelled from the birth canal within seconds.

Once the kitten is free of the birth canal, the queen will lick the membranes from its face and body, drying it and massaging its chest, as she rolls it over and over.

Each kitten is born attached to its own placenta by the umbilical cord. The placenta is normally produced immediately following the kitten's emergence from the uterus. Once the kitten's face is cleaned, and when the dam perceives her new baby to be breathing normally, the queen will chew the umbilical cord in two, often eating the placenta as she does so.

Queens usually eat the placenta as they remove it from the kitten.

Placenta Eating

Some breeders attempt to prevent a female from consuming her placentas. They believe that eating the tissue promotes vomiting and they watch the delivery carefully, eagerly trying to snatch every placenta away from the queen. I believe that the placentas cause the queen no harm, and it is a mistake to interfere with her natural instincts to eat them.

I have heard other breeders' opinions, claiming that the placental tissue contains hormones, and its consumption promotes heavier milk production and quicker uterine emptying. I doubt that the placental tissue has significant influence on either of those physiological activities, but I recommend allowing her to consume them if she wishes. Sometimes she ignores the placenta, and it is necessary to clamp and sever the umbilical cords (see The Placenta, page 85).

Labor Resumption

When she is satisfied that her new kitten is well and breathing normally, she may push the kitten to a nipple and encourage it to nurse. Uterine contractions continue to align the kittens in preparation for birth. When the next fetus is in an

Persian neonatal kitten, placenta still attached.

Kitten with placenta attached.

appropriate position, she will momentarily ignore the first-born and repeat the delivery performance.

The duration of Stage II labor before the presentation of the first kitten is irrelevant unless it exceeds one hour. The time lapse between births likewise ranges from a few minutes to an hour. A queen doesn't watch the clock, and there is no cause for alarm unless she is in hard labor for an hour without producing a kitten. If that occurs, call your veterinarian.

Variations

These are normal variations seen in queening. For instance, some multiparous queens display virtually none of the Stage I labor signs. They may hop from your lap, eat a snack, retire to their nest, and deliver their kittens. Others will hide for a week before delivery, then demand complete privacy during parturition.

Some queens insist on cleaning and nursing every kitten before labor is resumed. They seem able to postpone Stage II labor until they are ready for another kitten. On occasion, kittens will be born in such rapid succession that human help is necessary to assure live kittens.

Time elements are quite variable. I have known feline parturition to take all night, without the loss of a single kitten, and without any human assistance. The times quoted herein are good average standards, but your cat will establish her own schedules. After her first litter, you will be more easily able to predict the future delivery times and activities.

Queens of the long-established or inbred varieties, which might include Siamese, Persian, and perhaps some of the Oriental shorthairs, make a community production of parturition. I have known a few that would probably have lost their entire litters without human assistance. They seem to have become more dependent on their breeders with every new generation. If you own queens of those more dependent breeds, the following discussion of dystocia will be of particular value to you.

Chapter Eight
Dystocia and Delivery Assistance

Types of Dystocia

Difficult or interrupted parturition is termed *dystocia.* Its cause may be either fetal or maternal.

Fetal Dystocia

Dystocia caused by the fetus is usually due to kitten size or physical anomalies. Sometimes a litter is composed of a single, gigantic kitten. The queen's anatomical structures are normal but the fetus is too large to fit. In those cases, a cesarean section is indicated.

Occasionally, fetal monsters are seen. They may have extra legs or two heads, or they might be two fetuses joined at the spine. Those monstra (see Monstra and other Congenital Deformities, page 103) are usually delivered by cesarean section, and most are stillborn.

Maternal Dystocia

Maternal dystocia causes are more numerous. They include immaturity of the queen, especially when she is bred on her first heat. Her skeletal structure is undeveloped, and the birth canal is too small to accommodate normal-size fetuses. Again, surgical intervention is sometimes necessary to relieve the dystocia.

Uterine inertia is unlikely in young, normal, healthy queens. In those that are past their prime breeding years, this condition becomes more prevalent. It is also commonly seen in undernourished

Finding a nipple with milk.

cats, or those suffering chronic illnesses. The problem is a lack of uterine tone or muscular strength. The queen exhibits all the expected signs of labor, but no kittens are born. Usually, she will not produce the normal hard abdominal muscular contractions, because the uterine contractions have not positioned a kitten into the birth canal.

Inertia is occasionally treated successfully with pituitary hormone injections. Before that therapy is initiated, the cat should be professionally examined and evaluated. Indiscriminate administration of pituitary hormones may be contraindicated in some situations. Sometimes cesarean sections are the only solution to uterine inertia, but queens experiencing the condition may be poor surgical risks.

Uterine fatigue is another cause of maternal dystocia. It may accompany delivery of a large litter. It is usually the result of prolonged labor and tiring of the uterine musculature, accompanied by fatigue of the abdominal muscles. The condition is seen more frequently in aging queens or those that are in poor nutritional status. Hormone injections may stimulate uterine contractions, but as in uterine inertia, they shouldn't be used until the cat has been examined by your veterinarian to assure that no other complicating conditions exist.

Sometimes, a cat experiencing uterine fatigue will deliver part of her litter, and appear outwardly to have finished her delivery. Several hours or a day later, she will deliver another kitten or two that are often stillborn. This is another example of the importance of a veterinary examination following normal parturition.

Uterine torsion is, as its name implies, a twisted uterus. I have never seen a case in cats, but have diagnosed a few cases in dogs. In this condition, the uterus becomes turned on its long axis, effectively sealing off the fetus exit from the womb. The queen may exhibit Stage I labor, but never show any signs of productive abdominal contractions. Breeders should be alert to stalled labor situations and seek veterinary help quickly.

Physical Assistance

Other dystocias are less dangerous, and may be easily relieved by the breeder. When it is obvious that the mother needs help delivering a

Now I've got it right!

kitten, assistance should be rendered as quickly as possible, and then the newborn should be returned to its mother.

A kitten may partially emerge from the birth canal, then remain there. If it stays in that position without progress for more than three or four minutes, you should act. With clean hands, using a dry washcloth, pinch and tear the membranes that cover the kitten's head, and gently wipe the membranes away from its face. With a dry cotton swab or the corner of the cloth, wipe the mucus from its mouth. Then watch closely for delivery progress. If the kitten still isn't expelled from the birth canal during the next three or four minutes, more assistance should be rendered. With a dry cloth, grasp the kitten's head and shoulders carefully, and apply gentle traction.

The direction of traction is very important. Feline birth canals are tipped downward and backward, and traction is most effective if exerted in a direction nearly parallel to the dam's pelvic canal. To understand that concept, picture the cat standing up. The appropriate direction of traction would be toward the floor at a point 3 or 4 inches (7.6–10.2 cm) behind her hind feet.

Once you have extracted the kitten from the birth canal, quickly remove any remaining membranes from its head and swab the fluid and mucus from its mouth. If the oral fluid is copious, apply light suction to the mucus by aspirating it with the sterile syringe. If the newborn is

A queen usually begins to clean her kittens as soon as they emerge from the birth canal.

squirming and breathing, place it in front of the dam and go back to your seat in the audience. She will finish cleaning the baby and will appreciate your help.

Another situation that occasionally requires assistance is a very rapid delivery. If kittens are born in such quick succession that the mother doesn't have time to clean

When necessary, apply gentle downward and backward traction to the shoulders of kitten.

and care for them adequately, your help is important. Pick the kittens up one by one, using a cloth. Clean the membranes from their heads and remove the fluid from their mouths as described above, then place them in front of the mother with the placental membranes still attached.

One useful type of CPR utilizes centrifugal force to help empty the kitten's respiratory tract of fluids.

CPR for Kittens

A major problem that can be relieved by the owner involves a kitten that has fluid retained in its lungs or upper respiratory tract. It may be an infant that spent too much time in the birth canal, or it may be a victim of rapid delivery with insufficient attention by its mother. Newborn kittens normally obtain their first air in short gasps, but if a kitten is observed gasping or blowing mucus bubbles from its nose for several minutes, it may need help.

First, free the mouth of fluids with a cotton swab, or the corner of a cloth, or by aspirating the fluid with the syringe. If the kitten still seems to be in distress, pick it up with a dry cloth and cradle it in your upturned palms. Hold it belly up, with its head away from you. Its head should be supported between your two index fingers. Hold your thumbs over its chest in a gentle, firm grip. Then, standing with your feet apart and your arms extended, swing the kitten in a wide arc beginning from the height of your waist. The arc should end between your legs, near the floor, behind your feet.

That swinging action creates centrifugal force that extrudes fluids from the kitten's lungs and windpipe. After two swings, wipe its nostrils, swab out its mouth with a cotton swab, and gently massage its chest for a moment or two. Repeat the procedure until the bubbling stops and the kitten is breathing normally. Usually once or twice is adequate.

If the kitten does not breathe after repeating the above procedure two or three times, prop its mouth open with a finger, and from a distance of several inches, blow into its mouth (see illustration). If the kitten still doesn't breathe, repeat all the procedures again. Even if no response is seen, continue cardiopulmonary resuscitation (CPR) efforts for at least a half hour before giving up.

Help oxygenate and stimulate breathing by blowing into the kitten's mouth from a few inches away.

Handling Neonates

During, and immediately following parturition, do not handle the kittens more than is necessary. Cats are the best mothers imaginable, and only on rare occasions will they abandon a kitten or a litter. When they do, it is often the result of too much human handling of their offspring at the time of birth. It is especially important to limit necessary handling to a single person. If other members of your family watch a delivery, they should do so at a respectable distance. Passing a newborn kitten from one person to another will upset the queen, and might even interrupt her labor.

When breeders and their families get the urge to handle kittens as they are born, or during their first two or three days of life, they must accept the fact that some queens will respond by abandoning the litter. By default, you will inherit total responsibility for raising the kittens (see Orphan Kittens, page 117). My advice is to suppress the urge, and leave the neonatal care to the dam,

at least until she has them all cleaned, counted, sorted, and nursing. After they are a couple of days old, she shouldn't object to having them picked up and admired, providing they are kept very near her in the process.

The Placenta

Kittens are contained within individual placental sacs. As the kittens are born, each kitten's placenta detaches from the uterus and is shed within minutes after the kitten is born. Placentas are physically attached to kittens by their umbilical cords, and both are extruded from the uterus by the same wave of contractions. Placentas are rarely retained in the wombs of domestic felines, but be alert. If possible, count the placentas as they are produced, to be sure that they number the same as the kittens in the litter. Placental retention, when it does occur, may be a source of uterine

If necessary, clamp, tie, and cut umbilical cords.

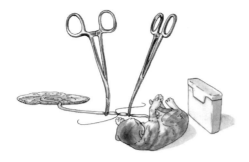

infection, and if suspected, you should contact your veterinarian.

If the mother chews through the umbilical cords within a short time after birth, there is no need for human action. If she leaves the placentas attached to the kittens for more than an hour, you may wish to intervene. Clamp the cords about 1 inch (2.5 cm) from the kittens' bellies with hemostat forceps. Tie the umbilical

cords tightly with dental floss. The ligatures (ties) should be placed against the kitten side of the forceps, and should be secured with two or three knots. Cut the ends of the dental floss ties close to the knots. Sever each umbilical cord between the hemostat and the placenta with a pair of sterile scissors. Remove the hemostat from the umbilical cord and dip the tied, kitten end of the severed cord into the jar of povidone iodine disinfectant. As previously mentioned, it is normal but not necessary for the mother to eat her kittens' placentas. If she ignores them, remove and dispose of them, but I don't advise taking the placentas away from her if she objects.

Breech or Posterior Births

Many kittens are born head first, but posterior presentations of the tail and hind legs are not uncommon. The significance of a posterior birth is that the kitten's head emerges from the birth canal last rather than first. The placenta may be detached from the uterus before the newborn's head has been delivered. In that event, quick delivery is imperative. If a kitten's tail and hind legs protrude from the birth canal for three or four minutes without complete delivery, apply traction. The procedure is the same as described in an anterior (head first) delivery, except that traction is applied to the hind legs and pelvis of the kitten instead of to its head. Be gentle!

A posterior presentation delivery should progress at a normal rate.

True breech births are uncommon. In mature queens they are not necessarily cause for alarm, but they do deserve your undivided attention. In a breech presentation, only the tail of a kitten emerges from the birth canal. The hind legs are tucked forward in the birth canal, and are not visible or accessible. Many such presentations proceed at a normal pace, and no assistance is necessary. However, if only a tail is apparent and the birth process is at a standstill for more than ten minutes, call your veterinarian. Do not attempt to deliver a breech kitten by applying traction to the tail or to the amniotic sac.

Certain dystocias or difficult births should inspire you to contact your veterinarian immediately. Emergencies that can't be or shouldn't be handled at home include nonproductive labor or a lengthy interruption of labor.

- If the queen shows signs of abdominal labor for an hour without producing a kitten, call the veterinarian.
- If a kitten remains lodged in the birth canal for more than ten minutes, and you are unable to successfully deliver it using the described technique, contact your veterinarian.
- If she delivers part of the litter, but there are obviously more to come,

and she stops labor for more than two hours, call her doctor.

- If she is bleeding from her birth canal, get on the phone.
- The presence of foul, green, or black discharge before the first kitten is born is another reason for phoning the veterinarian. (Subsequent to the birth of the first kitten, a greenish fluid is normally seen.)

Parturition Completion

When parturition is finished, the queen will usually begin to clean herself, and may take a quick stroll to her water dish. Usually, if no resumption of Stage II labor signs are seen for two hours, you can assume she is finished. Her appetite will return to normal within a day. If you suspect that a kitten or placenta has been retained within the womb, schedule an examination with your veterinarian, as soon as possible.

Even when all goes well, and the delivery proceeds uneventfully, it is advisable to have the new mother examined by your veterinarian as soon as practical after delivery, perhaps after she has spent the first quiet day with her family.

Many veterinarians will come to your home to check the dam and litter. That arrangement is preferred because it will minimize exposure of the kittens to other animals, and the queen will be more at ease in her own home. The experienced fingers of a veterinary clinician can usually determine whether or not all kittens have been delivered. At the same time, her mammae may be examined for the presence of abnormalities, including mastitis. An injection of pituitary hormone may be given to help evacuate the uterus of fluid and placental shreds. If you wish to avail yourself of a home visit, be sure to discuss it with your veterinarian well in advance of the need.

Chapter 9
Cesarean Section

Most cats have little difficulty in parturition, and feline pregnancies rarely end in surgery. Because rare circumstances are encountered when a cesarean section is necessary, it is best to be prepared. Your veterinarian should be kept advised of the anticipated queening date, and if unavailable, the doctor will give you a referral to another surgeon who will be able to help if needed.

gressive dystocias discussed previously, the veterinarian should be contacted immediately. Don't wait till morning to see if nature will resolve the problem. The doctor will undoubtedly ask you to take the queen to the animal hospital where a physical examination and evaluation will follow. If a cesarean section is indicated, it will be done as soon as practical.

Who Is Qualified to Perform a Cesarean?

All veterinarians who practice companion animal medicine are usually willing and able to perform cesarean sections. Such surgical training is universally taught in veterinary colleges, and most small animal clinicians have the opportunity to do such surgery on a routine basis. If your veterinarian does not practice surgery, he or she will refer you to a surgeon, but in general, you need not seek out a specialist.

When you detect a delivery complication, such as one of the nonpro-

Risk Factors

Certain risk factors are inherent in any surgical procedure. Healthy, strong cats are excellent surgical patients and unless there are complications, cesarean risks are minimal. It is important that you, as the breeder and owner, understand the risks to your queen as well as to the kittens. When the presurgical physical examination is completed, your veterinarian will have assessed the risks involved, and if that assessment is not made clear to you, ask questions.

The surgeon will attempt to lower risks by stabilization of the patient prior to and during surgery. You should be prepared to give the queen's complete medical history, including any previous anesthesia administered. Her breeding history is critically important. That information should address her breeding date, previous pregnancies, sizes of litters, the time when Stage I and Stage II labor began, the queen's diet during pregnancy, dietary supplements, loss of kittens in previous litters, recent illnesses, and accidents or injuries to her pelvic region.

The doctor may draw a small blood sample to check her white cell count, state of anemia, blood glucose, kidney function, and, perhaps, calcium level. This information is part of the risk assessment that will supply vital information relative to stabilization to minimize risk. In cases where patient risks are deemed to be significant, the surgeon may choose local, instead of general, anesthesia. Warmed intravenous fluid adminis-

All right, we chopped this one down.

tration may be indicated to correct preexisting deficiencies. Multiple electrolytes including calcium are sometimes added to the solutions. Whole blood transfusion may also be indicated in certain situations.

I have seen high risk cases, when the queen was in critical condition, quite depressed, or moribund, and to improve her chances of survival, an ovariohysterectomy was the best option. That operation may mean the loss of some kittens or the entire litter, but when the queen is in such critical condition, the fetuses are often dead before the operation is begun. Those kinds of situations are rarely encountered in managed cat breeding programs, but unfortunately, veterinarians are faced with them, and they bear mentioning.

Importance of Surgical Timing

The need for surgical intervention in parturition is rarely recognized until the queen is in Stage II labor. That means there is no time to spare! When required, all cesarean operations must be treated as emergencies. Delay may account for kitten deaths and higher risks to the dam.

Risks are always minimized when surgical needs are recognized early and actions are taken quickly. Animals that have become weak and exhausted by prolonged labor present higher surgical risks. If dystocias are ignored until fetuses die, the queens become toxic from absorp-

tion of decaying fetal tissue and are always poor surgical candidates.

Operations done during regular working hours always proceed smoother than those required at night or on weekends, but in my experience, most cesareans are done between midnight and 3 A.M. Because of the cooperative, uninterrupted efforts of both owners and veterinarians, late night operations probably present no higher risk than those done during the day.

Veterinarians usually have staff on call to assist in those midnight operations, but in some cases, breeders may be asked to help out. That possibility is discussed below.

Anesthesia

Anesthesia risk is minimized by the surgeons' knowledge and experience with their favorite anesthetic agents. The many products available today provide the surgeon with several choices of types and routes of administration. In short, there are risks in any procedure, but if the surgeon has been advised in advance of the possible need, arrangements have been made for assistance, and the patient is strong and healthy, they should not be cause for worry.

Surgical Technique

Although the operation is in the hands of a veterinary surgeon, it is wise to be aware of the basic ele-ments of the surgical procedure. The intricacies of a cesarean operation vary from surgeon to surgeon. No two will be done identically, and I don't intend to try to describe the best or only procedure.

After examination, a preanesthetic agent may be given to the cat. Its abdomen may then be shaved, and the instruments, drapes, gowns, gloves, and other equipment are made ready. A heated receiving box or incubator is usually situated near the surgical table, and a good supply of sterile towels are unwrapped.

The anesthetic agent is administered, either by injection or inhalation. Often an endotracheal tube is positioned in the cat's windpipe to allow oxygen to be administered during the procedure. The queen is secured on her back on the table that is often heated to prevent loss of body temperature during the operation. Her shaved abdomen is then prepared with antiseptic agents while the surgeon scrubs and dons a gown, cap, mask, and gloves.

Most veterinary surgeons employ instruments that monitor surgical patients' heartbeats and body temperatures continuously. In feline cesarean sections, body temperatures often drop precipitously, due to the large mass of tissue exposed to room temperature, and the small body mass of the patient. That eventuality is usually compensated by table heaters and by warming the patient immediately following the operation.

When helping with cesarean surgery, keep well away from the surgical field.

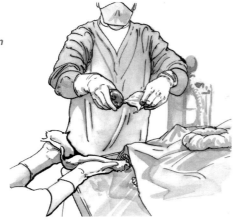

The table, instrument tray, and cat's abdomen are covered with sterile drapes. The surgeon makes a skin incision exactly on the midline, running from front to back, between the mammary glands. The length of the incision varies according to need, but will usually be about 3 inches (7.6 cm). If it is made precisely on the midline, there is only one other layer of tissue to incise to gain entry to the abdomen.

The gravid uterus is then lifted from the abdomen and laid on top of the drape. Its horns will each be about 2½ inches (6.4 cm) in diameter, and its walls will be quite turgid, stretched tightly over the fetuses. When both horns and part of the body of the uterus are exposed, an incision is made through the body of the uterus, on the midline, close to the point where it divides into horns.

The fetus closest to the uterine body is then squeezed backward, and out through the incision. Its face is immediately wiped off with a sterile sponge or towel, and the kitten and its placenta are dropped into the towel that is held in the waiting hands of the surgical assistant.

The remaining fetuses are likewise delivered and turned over to the assistant, whose duties are discussed below. When all are delivered, the uterine incision is sutured, that organ is replaced into the abdomen, and the abdominal incision is closed.

The operation usually progresses very rapidly. Speed is important to conserve body temperature, minimize anesthetic use, and hasten recovery. If you find yourself assisting in surgery, you will find that you scarcely have time to clean and massage one kitten before another is waiting for your attention.

Surgical Assistance

The duties of an assistant are simple and easy. When a kitten is dropped into your towel-covered hands, you must quickly remove the amniotic sac from its head, swab its mouth free of mucus and fluid with the corner of the towel, rub its chest a few seconds, and prepare to catch the next one.

When time allows, go back over each of the neonates and be sure they are breathing easily, dry and massage chests, and clamp umbilical cords. No two surgeons are alike, and each has little idiosyncrasies and peculiar ideas that must be accommodated. One important thing to remember is that you should *never reach over the surgical area.* The area covered by sterile drapes is the exclusive bailiwick of the surgeon's gloved hands. Stay well back, and wait for the surgeon to hand a kitten to you.

Once the kittens are delivered and the queen is waking, they will likely be dismissed and sent home to your care. It is important to get them back into their normal environment as soon as possible. Many veterinarians only keep cesarean patients in the hospital if there are complications that require intensive care or therapeutic measures.

How can you resist this Birman kitten?

Postsurgical Care

Usually, surgical recovery is uneventful. Sometimes the skin is sutured with material that is absorbed; other surgeons prefer to use sutures or clips that must be removed. Specific written instructions relative to aftercare and return visits should be given to you when the pet is released.

On rare occasions, a cat will worry at her skin incision, removing sutures and opening the wound. That means you should look at the surgical site several times a day for the first few days. If bleeding, swelling, or tissue discoloration is evident, call the veterinarian immediately.

Care for cesarean-delivered kittens is no different than for those delivered naturally. Generally, feline dams are so self-sufficient that little care is needed for the litter for several weeks.

Chapter 10
Lactation

The queen's milk provides both nutrition and immunity to neonatal kittens. The few days of colostral milk production provides the kittens with virtually all their protective antibodies that must serve them until they can be vaccinated at about weaning time.

The two-month period following parturition is probably the time of greatest nutritional stress on a breeding queen. Normal queens will often lose a fourth of their body weights between parturition and weaning time, six or eight weeks later. Large litters of active kittens take their toll on the dam's nutritional surplus, even in the best managed catteries. To accommodate the increased demand, breeders are advised to review the previous discussion on nutrition.

About 24 hours before delivery, a queen's appetite drops considerably. Within a day after queening, her dietary intake should approach the normal maintenance level, then rapidly rise until the kittens are taking in solid food.

Nutritional Recommendations

Supplements are not usually needed or advised. Cats usually love to drink milk, especially whole milk. Well-meaning breeders are sometimes tempted to give milk to nursing queens, but that practice is definitely discouraged! Cow's milk or goat's milk, regardless of the butterfat content, shouldn't be fed to cats, especially lactating dams. The result of milk consumption is usually diarrhea that causes electrolyte imbalances, and loss of condition.

Rich meats are also contraindicated. Meat scraps or 100 percent

Bengals. Lots of spots.

meat products do not provide balanced nutrition for cats. They fail to provide the necessary vitamins, minerals, and other nutritional elements needed for lactating queens.

Nutritional quality of foods recommended for lactating queens is the same as during growth and breeding. Use only premium quality foods that have the AAFCO feeding trial statement on the label. Foods carrying that statement that are recommended for all life stages of cats should provide good nutrition to your nursing queen. Free-choice dry foods may be supplemented with two or three meals a day of premium canned products. About the only dietary difference between a maintenance diet and a lactating diet is the amount consumed. During peak lactation, a nursing queen's food intake will increase from two to four times her maintenance level. That compares to an increase of only about 50 percent above maintenance at the time of parturition.

When kittens become interested in solid food, usually at three to four weeks of age, the dam's intake will begin to decrease, and shortly after weaning it will approximate her maintenance level. Usually, as the kittens go to new homes, the dam's dietary intake is voluntarily reduced without any action on your part.

Most queens will continue to nurse their kittens periodically until they are physically removed from her. As you observe your queen eating less dry food, you should gradually reduce the amount of canned food you offer. Within a week after weaning the kittens, the queen should be fed her normal maintenance diet.

Exercise

Feline motherhood transforms even the most playful cats into matronly role models. They seem to cherish their maternal duties and spend practically all their time curled up with their babies. Short trips to the litter box, food pans, and water bowls are their only diversion for the first two or three weeks. As the kittens' eyes open and they become more mobile, the dam will begin to leave them for longer periods.

Some breeds are quite athletic, and their exercise habits differ greatly from the more sedentary breeds. You can expect queens that were previously animated and playful to resume their activities very gradually after parturition. Exercise should be encouraged, but not forced, on lactating queens. If your cat liked to fetch or play with a ball on a string, begin those play periods again when the kittens are about three weeks old.

The same general idea applies to grooming. Your time is well spent when combing and brushing your feline friend, and it shouldn't be neglected during pregnancy or lactation. It may, however, be suspended during the first couple of weeks following parturition.

Special Care of Lactating Queens

Lactating queens that have been maintained on good nutrition throughout their lives usually require little special attention at this time. In spite of the severe stress they undergo, they usually manage to keep themselves quite clean and care for their own needs very well.

Occasionally, queens become so involved with their kittens that they retain urine and feces. That eventuality is usually managed by placing a litter box very close to the nest, and changing the litter daily. If, after the first couple of days, the queen doesn't leave the kittens to use her box, remove the kittens from the nest for 15 or 20 minutes once or twice a day. She will leave the nest to look for her brood, and hopefully will use the box while out. In some cases, it is easier to lift the queen from the nest and take her into another room. Even if she runs immediately back to her kittens, you will have an opportunity to observe her standing and moving.

A queen's dietary intake must increase dramatically during the first several days of lactation. To ensure that she eats as much and as frequently as necessary, move her food and water dishes to the immediate nest box area, and monitor her food intake as closely as possible.

A few days after delivery, check her tail hair and the coat of the perineal region. If the hair is stained and matted, it can be carefully clipped off with blunt scissors or cleaned with soap and water. Most cat breeders clip the hair of those regions very short prior to queening. The only precaution to observe when washing a lactating queen is to be sure only mild soaps are used, and that they are completely rinsed from her skin. Remember that cats are fastidious groomers, and she will lick the washed area as soon as you finish.

At least once a day, examine the queen's mammae. They should be quite full and distended part of the time, and equally empty after the litter has nursed. If one particular gland remains distended when others are flaccid, it may indicate a problem (see Mastitis, page 97).

Mammary abrasions are routinely seen after the kittens' toenails begin to grow. When the kittens are two weeks old, their nails can be trimmed to minimize the mammary trauma. I do not advise applying any topical medication to the nursing queen's mammary glands. As kittens aggressively nurse the nipples, they also lick and suck on the skin surrounding them. Any medication applied to those areas will be consumed by the neonates, and may cause serious digestive problems or drug reactions.

During the nursing period, kittens should also be periodically examined by the breeder (see Neonatal Examinations, page 103).

Chapter 11
Postparturient Problems

Postparturient complications are uncommon following a normal feline delivery, but you should be alerted to the danger signs of certain conditions.

Hemorrhage

Slightly blood-tinged fluids are normally seen at the time of delivery; however, hemorrhage from the birth canal immediately following delivery is a sign of a serious complication. It represents an emergency, and therapy must not be delayed. Call your veterinarian and transport the cat to the animal hospital immediately.

Uterine Prolapse

Feline uterine prolapse is described in veterinary literature, but its occurrence is extremely rare.

When a uterus prolapses, it appears as a significant mass of very vascular, pink tissue extending outward from the birth canal. It constitutes a medical, or sometimes surgical, emergency and your veterinarian should be contacted immediately.

Vomiting and Diarrhea

Vomiting and diarrhea episodes sometimes follow queening. Those conditions are usually transitory and have no lasting effect or significance. Temporary digestive upsets are often related to placenta eating as well as the consumption of kitten excretions. You will find that the queen's feces takes on a bronze or green coloration following parturition, that, too, has no particular significance. If diarrhea or vomiting persists for more than a day, consult with your veterinarian.

Mastitis

Mastitis, or mammary gland infection, is uncommon in felines, but you should be on the lookout for it. When it occurs, the affected gland will be warmer than the others; it is

ial will be revealed when the queen is examined following delivery. If the clinician has any doubt, X rays or ultrasound imaging will help diagnose the condition. Therapy may only necessitate the use of hormone injections, or, in some cases, surgery is required.

Mastitis is a serious, painful condition that demands immediate veterinary attention.

sometimes inflamed, and tender to the touch. If discovered, take the cat's temperature with a rectal thermometer, and call your veterinarian. Systemic antibiotics may reverse the condition within a few days. If ignored, the infection will cause a generalized illness that will affect her milk production and threaten her health and that of the kittens. Although early mastitis signs do not necessarily constitute an emergency, do not delay obtaining professional examination and therapy! Indiscriminate use of oral or injectable antibiotics should be avoided. Mastitis may not respond to the antibiotics given, and kittens may suffer adversely from drugs given to the dam during lactation.

Retained Kittens

Retained placentas are very uncommon in felines, but retained kittens are frequently seen. Sometimes those retained fetuses undergo mummification and remain in the womb for weeks. Usually retention of fetal or placental mater-

Eclampsia

Eclampsia is usually a postparturient disease, although cases have been recorded immediately prior to delivery. It is seen more commonly in dogs than cats, but it warrants discussion as a point of information. Eclampsia, or hypocalcemic tetany, is a metabolic, physiological phenomenon. Its occurrence is related to the high demand for calcium for the formation of fetal skeletons and for milk production.

Its signs are very obvious, and can't be missed by observant breeders. The cat will display progressive symptoms of incoordination, staggering, twitching, and even convulsions. The early signs will be overlooked if the cat isn't seen away from its brood. That is one of many reasons for insisting that the queen take a brief respite from her nursing duties once or twice daily.

If you suspect eclampsia, contact your veterinarian. Untreated animals may progress to convulsions, and possibly death. Treatment success is very predictable and recovery is usually quick. Calcium solutions are administered by injection,

Birman kittens having no trouble with solid food.

and the cat will return to normal within minutes.

Metritis

Metritis refers to a uterine inflammation or infection. It is often caused by tissue trauma associated with prolonged deliveries and dystocias. Retained placentas, retained kittens, and poor hygiene practices in the cattery are other causes of the problem. This condition often takes several days to develop, but when recognized, it must be treated as an emergency.

One of the first signs of metritis might be a foul vaginal discharge, but often the queen's cleaning habits prevent the discharge from being obvious. As the disease progresses, her body temperature will increase, her appetite will be diminished, and lethargy will be noted. As her milk production is decreased, kittens will cry from hunger.

If any combination of those symptoms are observed, take her temperature and call your veterinarian. Antibiotic therapy may be effective, especially early in the course of the disease.

In addition to being a serious, potentially fatal disease of the queen, metritis has a tremendous impact on the health and life of the kittens. Even early in the course of the disease, toxic wastes from the infected womb may be absorbed into the queen's bloodstream. From there they find their way into the milk, and kittens can suffer from secondary toxemia. They will show signs of lethargy, appetite loss, and weight loss. Anorexia (loss of appetite) may cause death within a day or two.

Hyperplastic Nipples

Hyperplastic nipples is another condition that is rarely seen in felines. It is usually the result of repeated trauma to the nipples over a long life of frequent kitten production. I have only observed it a couple of times, and only in older queens that were not part of a management program. Their owners undoubtedly didn't feed the kittens and the queens nursed them for extended periods of time. The signs are rough, scarlike tissue masses that cause enlargement of nipples.

Milk Duct Atresia

Sometimes an individual mammary gland will appear distended and unused, when compared to the other glands. One possible cause is mastitis in that gland, but another possibility is a plugged nipple. Kittens try to nurse from it, but when no milk is forthcoming, they move to another gland.

If you suspect atresia, try to squeeze a drop of milk from the nipple. If unable to do so, the duct leading from the milk-producing tissue to the tip of the nipple is probably occluded. Usually the condition can go untreated without complications, because the milk production will stop, the swelling will subside, and the gland will become inactive. Queens usually have more functional mammae than kittens, so the loss of one gland isn't terribly important. If you wish to have the duct opened, telephone your veterinarian.

Chapter 12
Neonatal Kitten Care

A healthy cat nursing a healthy litter is the picture of peace and contentment. Given an even break, most newborn kittens require no human interaction. They are typically tough, resilient little creatures with very aggressive appetites. I have seen them still wet from birth, dragging their placentas by the umbilical cords, as they fight for a nipple. When only hours old, they respond to their mother's voice and nudging. They seem to spend much of their time piled in a mound against their dam's belly, but when awakened, their immediate reaction is to find their way to the source of her warm, nourishing milk.

Cats are incomparable mothers. I have had experience with virtually all domestic animals and their young, but none compare with the pride and satisfaction displayed by a nursing queen. Purring contentedly, she washes and massages the kittens repeatedly with her rough, papilla-covered tongue. Within a day or two, their coats shine and their immaculate bodies appear to have just emerged from a grooming parlor. Within a few weeks, she will begin to teach them manners, hunting techniques, and games. If facilities are available, she will even litter train her babies.

Most queens spend well over 90 percent of every day with their brood for at least two weeks. About the only time they leave the nest is to take care of their own nutritional and excretory needs. A good mother licks her brood's abdominal and urogenital areas, stimulating and consuming their excretions. She examines them several times daily, methodically sorting out the one that needs grooming or cleaning the most.

For this reason, among others, the best way to care for the daily needs of a litter of newborn kittens is to assure the good health and nutri-

Queens begin to clean their kittens as soon as they have been born.

When uncomfortable with their surroundings, dams often move their kittens.

tion of their mother throughout her life, but especially from the time of breeding until the kittens are weaned.

Kitten Moving

One of the most common questions I have been asked by cat breeders pertains to a queen moving her litter. Invariably the problem stemmed from a lack of quiet and privacy. Cats don't mind visitors, but access to their queening nest should be restricted for at least the first two weeks. During that time, visiting hours in the maternity ward should be limited to a couple of trips a day, and no one should handle the kittens except a designated adult owner.

When disturbed by too much noise or confusion, a cat will usually move her brood to another location. Unfortunately, the new location may be totally inappropriate. Favorite hiding places are under beds, in the corners of closets, behind furniture, and other nearly inaccessible places.

Admittedly, many queens are not particular, and will allow the family to handle her kittens at will. She may even seem to invite your admiration and attention. Those traits are wonderful, and if they surface in your queen, you are very fortunate. However, until you have been through the kitten-raising experience at least once or twice, it is best to furnish her with a secluded nest in which to raise her litter.

If your cat is a long-haired breed, and if you have not done so previously, trim the hair from her belly to allow freer kitten access to her nipples. Consider also trimming the hair from her perineal area to facilitate her cleaning chores.

Kitten Color-Code Identification

Shortly after birth, you should pick up each kitten in turn and examine it for defects. While performing that examination you should mark the kittens for future identification and record keeping. Marking the kittens is unnecessary if nature has given them individualized color patterns. It becomes very important, however, in breeds like the Siamese, who are all born white. Kittens of many other breeds are also nearly identical when born, with their individualized coat patterns developing after several weeks.

The best marking product I know is fingernail polish. Obtain a different color of nail polish for each kitten. Paint several rear toenails of each kitten with its own color, and put a spot of a corresponding color on separate pages of a notebook. As the kittens are examined, they can be named or numbered, with the appropriate name or number recorded on the page beside that kitten's color.

Nail polish markings should be renewed every week until the kittens are sold. If one is spoken for before weaning time, the sale can also be noted on the kitten's record.

Neonatal Examinations

Another breeder responsibility is to perform a cursory examination of each kitten when they are a few hours old. This should take place as soon after parturition as practical, once the queen has cleaned her brood and is nursing them. This brief but important exam is intended to identify congenital problems such as physical deformities. It serves to establish and record each kitten's sex, birth weight, respiratory health, strength, and nursing aggressiveness. The data recorded at this neonatal period will often alert the conscientious breeder to future problems and perhaps save a kitten's life. When the kittens are a few hours old, as you take each one from the dam to mark its toe-

nails with fingernail polish, look it over carefully.

Balinese female and kittens.

Monstra and Other Congenital Deformities

Birth of a fetal monstrum (monster) occurs in most breeds occasionally. *Monstra* (plural of monstrum) are newborn animals with congenital anomalies that are greatly pronounced and evident. They include extra heads or duplication of other body parts, absence of extremities or organs, and many other physical abnormalities. Monstra are often stillborn or die shortly after birth. Some may survive longer if provided special support.

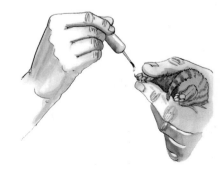

Identify kittens with different colors of nail polish.

The breeder should gently examine kittens shortly after birth.

Swimmer kittens or *flat kittens* have flattened or compressed chests. As infants, they typically lie flat on their abdomens, with their legs extended to each side on the same plane as their bodies. Some swimmers seem to recover and are placed in pet homes. Others retain the flat conformation and can't compete with siblings. Many are destroyed when diagnosed, to reduce competition for milk and to minimize stress on the dam. *Any kitten with chest compression should be neutered at maturity and eliminated from the gene pool of the breed.*

How much did I weigh last week?

Owners should inspect all kittens for umbilical hernias, which appear as small soft, spherical enlargements under the abdominal skin at the navel. Some swelling is normal at the umbilical cord's point of attachment, but if the swelling is soft, and larger than other kittens' in the litter, make note of it. Some kittens have what appear to be small hernias, but within a week the swellings are gone and the abdomens appear normal. If the umbilical skin has parted, or if any blood or serum is evident, consider it an emergency and call your veterinarian immediately. If the skin is sealed and no tenderness is apparent, you should alert the veterinarian to the situation, but it is probably not an emergency. True umbilical hernias continue to remain enlarged, and at some time in the future (rarely before six months of age) they will require surgical correction.

Check legs and feet for deformities. In some breeds, extra toes (polydactyly) are found. If that condition is discovered, check your breed standards to see if it constitutes a major fault. If so, that kitten should be considered only as a pet, to be neutered at maturity, and removed from the gene pool of the breed.

Tail kinks are faults in most breeds, and should be noted for future reference. In the Manx, breed standards are specific relative to tail type and length.

Note that the kittens' eyelids are sealed shut. Their ear canals are closed as well. They will open sometime during the second week of life. Irreparable damage will be done to the eyes if you attempt to unseal the eyelids.

Open every mouth and check for cleft palates. That rare recessive genetic fault is occasionally seen in breeds that have been inbred for several generations. The condition is easily identified as a separation or split extending along the midline of the palate. Some clefts extend the entire length of the palate; some are abbreviated and only reach a short distance. If you suspect a cleft palate, make note of the kitten's identity and watch it nurse. If milk bubbles from its nose as it swallows, if it has difficulty nursing, swallows air, and cries a lot, your veterinarian should be contacted immediately. Even if the kitten seems to progress normally, it should receive special attention when the litter is seen by your veterinarian.

While you have the kitten's mouth open, look at its oral mucous membranes that cover the structures within the mouth. The gums, tongue, and lips should be moist and vibrant pink. Pale, gray, or blue-gray membranes are signs of serious problems. They may be indications of anemia, or lack of adequately oxygenated blood. Bluish, pale membranes are extremely important because they may indicate respiratory or cardiac insufficiencies, and your veterinarian should be consulted. If in doubt as to the normal color of oral mucous membranes,

compare the kittens to one another, and to the dam.

I can see, I can see.

Check the other end of the kitten. *Atresia ani* (lack of an anal opening) is another very rare condition that is sometimes treatable if discovered immediately.

Lay the kitten in your palm and observe its respiratory rate and depth. This part of the exam is usually difficult for the owner, because neonatal respiration differs significantly from that of an adult. If its breathing seems labored, rapid, and shallow, or choppy in nature, it may have an airway blockage resulting in inability to oxygenate. If you aren't sure, compare the kitten's respiratory character to that of its siblings. A kitten with breathing difficulty will probably also be uncomfortable, crying, restless, and struggling. Possible causes for *dyspnea* (difficult breathing) are many and varied. One of the first thoughts in a newborn is mucus or fluid remaining in the upper respiratory tree. Blowing mucus bubbles from the nostrils is a sign that fluid still exists in the upper respiratory system. The CPR technique described previously (see page 84) should be used to help eliminate that fluid.

A relatively uncommon, but very important feline congenital deformity is persistent ductus arteriosis (PDA). In unborn animals, there is a natural shunt (ductus arteriosis) that connects the arteries carrying blood to the body, with vessels transporting blood to the lungs (remember the lungs aren't functional until after birth). That arterial shunt will normally close at birth, but sometimes it remains open. When a ductus arteriosis persists after birth, the kitten's growth and progress is slowed. Sometimes affected neonates have breathing difficulties, rapid heartbeats, and pale oral membranes. Many kittens with PDA are weak, lethargic, and anorectic, and soon die. Others survive, but they are usually smaller and less energetic than their siblings. Surgical treatment may be possible, but is expensive. If a single kitten in a litter seems to do poorly, have it examined by a professional before you begin home therapy.

After your examination is finished, as you replace each kitten into the nest, lay it on its back and watch its righting reflex. It should roll quickly onto its chest and immediately begin seeking the warm safety of its dam or siblings.

Healthy newborns' coats should be soft and clean. Excessive skin wrinkles in newborn kittens are abnormal. When they occur, they are often signs of dehydration. Depending on the state of dehydration, kittens can be treated, but first have the kitten examined by a veterinarian. A professional examination and perhaps a lab test will help to prescribe the type and duration of treatment needed. Very minor dehydration may correct itself in aggressively nursing kittens. Professional treatment for dehydration may involve oral fluid administration or injections of sterile electrolyte solutions.

Lack of complete hair cover or sparse coats may indicate premature birth. Premature kittens are weak and do not nurse well. When discovered, supplemental bottle feeding or stomach tube feeding may be necessary to save them. Suspected premature kittens should be examined and evaluated by your veterinarian to rule out internal congenital deformities that may complicate the picture.

Weight

Birth weights should be recorded, and I advise you to weigh the kittens daily until weaned to ascertain their rate of gain. Kittens normally weigh between 3 and 4 ounces (84–112 g) at birth. After the first day, they should gain at least ½ ounce (14 g) each day. Be sure that you check their weights at the same time each day. It is common for a robust kitten to weigh 1 pound (0.5 kg) at one month or five weeks of age, having quadrupled its birth weight in that short time period.

Accurate scales are available at pet supply stores and catalog order houses. Dietetic scales that weigh in grams are sufficiently accurate, but grocery produce-type scales have a wide margin of error.

Body Temperature

If it becomes necessary to take a kitten's temperature, be advised that for the first few weeks of life, they mimic cold-blooded animals, with their body temperatures responding to those of their environment. Normal kittens' temperatures at birth are about 97°F (36°C). Those temperatures should increase gradually, reaching 101.5°F (38.5°C) by the end of the third week of life.

To take their temperatures, use an *oral stubby* type human thermometer. Be sure the mercury is shaken down below 90°F (32°C). Lubricate it with petroleum jelly and insert it ½ inch (1.3 cm) into the rectum. Keep a gentle but firm hold on both the kitten and the thermometer during the minute or two it remains in the rectum.

There is a new generation of human infant thermometers that may be adaptable for use in kittens. They instantly record temperatures from within the ear canal of humans. If interested, I encourage you to try one. Be sure to correlate the new instrument's readings with those of an old-fashioned rectal thermometer on a few kittens before you adopt their use. And remember, kittens' ear canals don't open until they are ten days old or older.

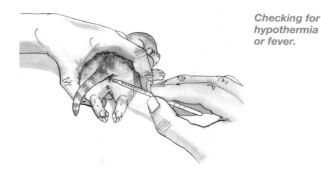

Checking for hypothermia or fever.

Sex Determination

Some breeders find it difficult to differentiate between the sexes at a very early age, but I think it is easiest the first few days of life.

View the neonatal kittens from the rear, with their tails elevated. The aperture of the female genitalia is immediately below her anus. The opening into the male prepuce is similar in appearance, but it is much lower, more distant from his anus. The testicles may not be discernible at birth, but within a week they can be seen and felt in the space between the anus and the prepuce orifice.

So what if we're cheating?

Eating Habits of Neonatal Kittens

For the first two weeks of life, kittens are usually nursing most of their waking moments. Like their parents, they catnap between their dozens of meals every day. Supplemental feeding of kittens during the first weeks of life is unnecessary if the mother is well and has ample milk, and if the kittens are clean, happy, eating well, and gaining weight. The mother's nutritional requirements continue to increase as her kittens grow. Her caloric intake increased by about 25 percent during gestation, and will increase another 25 percent by the time the kittens are weaned. Those figures are average, not literal. They depend on litter size and the quality of food being fed.

Feline colostrum, produced for about three days, differs significantly from normal feline milk. Even after the colostral production has passed,

queen's milk continues to change in content throughout the six to eight weeks of lactation. Colostrum contains about 88 percent water, whereas milk contains 82 percent. The protein content of colostrum is about 4 percent, and that level grows to over 6 percent as lactation progresses. Fat content increases from slightly over 3 percent to 5.5 percent at the end of lactation. Milk mineral levels also fluctuate during lactation. These facts should serve to remind you that colostrum and natural mother's milk is the best diet for kittens until they are able to digest solid food.

If kittens seem to be nursing well, but do not gain at the expected rate, don't hesitate to supplement their diet with a commercial feline milk replacement formula. It should be fed through one of the feline nursing devices that is fitted with an appropriate size nipple. Use of a syringe to force-feed tiny kittens may be an acceptable procedure in experienced hands, but it is fraught with dangers when attempted by a novice. If force-feeding is necessary, it is sometimes safer to use a stomach tube. Before force feeding a kitten, consult with your veterinarian who can instruct you in proper kitten feeding techniques.

Kittens vary in their acceptance of solid food, but most will begin eating softened, moist commercial foods sometime between three and six weeks of age. They should not be forced to do so at a certain age, nor should they be separated from their mother before she weans them, even if they are eating cat food well.

A good way to start the kittens on solid food is to mix a tablespoonful of a premium, canned kitten food or strained meat baby food with a similar amount of dry baby cereal. Moisten the mixture with feline milk replacer until it reaches the consistency of thick pea soup. Put that mixture in a saucer and dip the kittens' muzzles into it. They will lick it from their whiskers and faces, and, once tasted, they will begin to try to lap it from the saucer. After two or three such training sessions, it will be unnecessary to dip their muzzles into the mixture. Once they have begun to eat voluntarily, decrease the milk replacer in the mixture, and increase the cereal and cat food.

Once they have become accustomed to a canned food and cereal mixture, soak some premium dry kitten food with milk replacer and mix it with the canned diet in place of the baby cereal. After they have fully accepted that mixture, begin increasing the amount offered at each meal, and feed it twice daily. At that time, make dry kitten food available to them, free-choice, and offer them a spoonful or two of canned kitten food twice a day.

How to Spot a Sick Kitten

There are several ways to monitor the health status of kittens. It is typical for kittens to lose a bit of weight their first day, but after a day or two of life, kittens should be round, firm, and fully packed. They should have

A kitten will lick semi-solid food from its whiskers and voluntary eating will follow.

moist noses, bright pink, moist tongues and lips, and supple skins. Their coats should be clean and well groomed, and they should squirm and wriggle when picked up. They should only cry when the mother steps on them, when they are handled by humans, or when they are rooted away from a nipple by a sibling. A kitten that cries continuously or frequently, for no apparent reason,

Kittens come with eyes and ears sealed.

may be in trouble. It may be injured or have colic or some other illness, but it needs attention.

If a kitten feels limp or flaccid when handled and lacks vigorous behavior, it is likely in trouble. Take immediate measures to identify the problem. Weak kittens may die in less than a day if no action is taken to correct their problems.

A dry-skinned kitten that feels thin or appears bloated may be in trouble. One that is too weak to compete successfully for a nipple or one that is found by itself, separated from the rest of the litter, should be watched carefully.

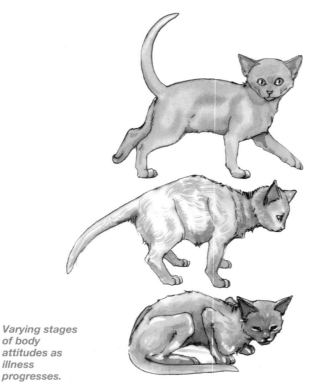

Varying stages of body attitudes as illness progresses.

A kitten that is ignored by the dam needs prompt attention. If the mother does not allow it to nurse, pushes it aside, and does not clean and minister to it, it is likely in big trouble. Tough as kittens are, they have practically no reservoirs of strength or nutrition to call upon when they are so young and tiny. It is always advisable to consult with your pet's doctor when you suspect illness in a kitten.

After nursing a few times, kittens' abdomens should be full but not distended. Kittens with distended or bloated abdomens cry and are usually seen wandering, apart from siblings. They may try to nurse, give up, and try another nipple. Bloated kittens usually demonstrate ineffective nursing, swallow air, and exhibit colic signs. Notes should be made and bloated kittens should receive professional evaluation as soon as possible.

Colic is a catchall term that is applied to practically any disorder that causes kittens to exhibit signs of digestive distress. There are many remedies for colic that may or may not work, depending on the cause of the condition. I recommend that you obtain a specific diagnosis of the cause of a bellyache before you administer any medicine to a kitten with colic. If you decide to try home remedies without benefit of specific diagnosis, be especially mindful of the intestinal absorptive rate of newborns compared to older kittens. Correct dosages of all medications are calculated by the weight and age. Drugs that are safe in kittens of one age and size may be fatal to younger or smaller animals.

Umbilical Cord Care

Usually, the umbilical cords require no attention after they are severed from the placenta. The short cord stubs will dry up and fall off, or will be chewed off by the mother, within a week or two after birth. If a cord appears swollen and inflamed and the kitten is restless, or if its abdomen is tender when touched, call your veterinarian immediately.

Eye Care

Kittens are born with their eyes sealed tightly shut. They usually open between the eighth and twelfth days of life. Their ear canals are also sealed at birth, and they open a few days after the eyes. Infrequently, a yellow or green discharge exudes from the eyelids of a kitten at about the time the lids separate. If that occurs, gently swab both eyes with a cotton ball that has been soaked with ophthalmic boric acid solution obtained from a pharmacy. That treatment should be repeated four or five times a day until no further discharge is seen. If the discharge does not diminish after two days of home treatment, call your veterinarian.

Less common is a tender swelling beneath the eyelids before the eyes

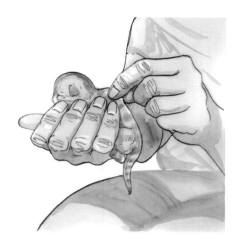

Checking a neonatal kitten for dehydration.

open. That may indicate an infection that is trapped under the sealed eyelids, and it is a good reason for a visit to the doctor. If you wish to try first aid before contacting your veterinarian, wash the eyes with cotton balls soaked in ophthalmic boric acid solution. Gentle, brisk rubbing of the eyelids may cause them to open, and they can then be cleaned as described above. Never pry or cut the eyelids apart; if the eyelids do not open with washing, make an early appointment with the kitten's doctor.

Hypoglycemia

Hypoglycemia (low blood sugar) can cause kittens to exhibit weakness, difficulty breathing, and crying. Those signs are also seen with dehydration, hypothermia, and trauma. If the cause of symptoms is in doubt, consult with your veterinarian. Laboratory tests can measure

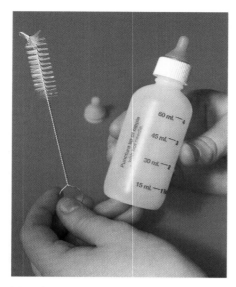

blood sugar and state of dehydration. Don't overlook the possibility of a kitten having been handled roughly or dropped by a child.

Eating Habits

Normal kittens with full stomachs are usually found sleeping in a cluster when not nursing.

Make notes about an individual kitten's eating behavior, whether it is aggressive or apathetic. If a kitten is found separated from its mother, make note on its record. If it is often separated, examine it closely; there is probably a reason. All kittens cry occasionally, and such crying is not noteworthy, but if one particular kitten cries frequently and the others do not, look it over. If a reasonable diagnosis isn't made by your examination, call for help.

Restless, crying kittens are probably hungry. If one is found in that state, squeeze a drop or two of milk from a nipple, and while the milk drops are suspended on the nipple's tip, introduce the nipple into the kitten's mouth and watch closely. The hungry kitten may have been shoved from a breast by a stronger sibling, and when it is allowed to nurse without competition, it will fill its stomach promptly.

If most of the brood are restless and crying or moving from nipple to nipple, the queen should be thoroughly examined. Take her temperature and check the milk flow from each gland. If her milk production is inadequate to meet kitten demand, review her diet, both quality and quantity, and have her examined. It is probably prudent to shop for bottles, nipples, and replacement formula as well.

Nursing Care for Sick Kittens

If force-feeding is necessary for any reason, consult with your veterinarian about the products to use, the frequency of feedings, quantity to feed, and the safest procedure to employ.

Hypothermia and hypoglycemia may be treated by providing supplemental warmth and oral administration of certain glucose-containing, electrolyte fluids. The electrolyte balance and specific glucose concentration in those fluids is very important. Oral fluid administration may be repeated frequently, according to need and response. I urge you not to give oral glucose or electrolytes without professional advice and instructions. Your veterinarian will probably make recommendations over the phone, and will help you acquire the appropriate fluids.

Commercial milk replacer may be obtained from pet supply houses. Its use may also aid in correcting hypoglycemia, hypothermia, and nutritional deficits. It can be fed by bottle and nipple, or it may be administered by stomach tube. All liquids must be warmed to the kitten's body temperature or slightly above. If using commercial milk-replacer products, adhere strictly to the label's dosage instructions. More serious fluid imbalances may be treated by your veterinarian using subcutaneous or intravenous glucose and electrolyte solutions.

Environmental Control

Whether you are treating a single sick kitten or the entire litter, the environment must be conducive to their recuperation. Heat lamps are dangerous and should never be used in a feline hospital room to provide warmth for kittens. There are several ways that the proper temperature can be maintained in a sick bed, but sunlamps or infrared lights are not among them.

The best place for a kitten before weaning is with its mother. If she rejects an ill kitten and pushes it from the nest, you must act as her

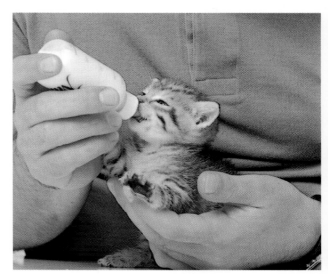

substitute. Groom it frequently with a dry cloth and stimulate its excretions by washing its belly and anal area with the corner of a damp washcloth or sponge. Keep it warm, and provide its nutrition.

If the rejected kitten is less than three weeks old, an incubator may

Not like mamma's milk, but it'll do.

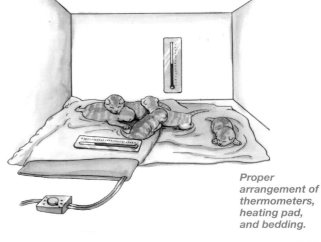

Proper arrangement of thermometers, heating pad, and bedding.

be needed. One can be fashioned from a small box and a heating pad wrapped several times with toweling or a flannel cloth. A small cat carrier also makes a good incubator. An integral part of any homemade incubator is an accurate, easily read thermometer. Before the sick kitten is introduced, adjust the pad's thermostat so that the floor of the incubator stays at 88 to 92°F (31°C–33.3°C) constantly. Be sure that there is ample floor space that is unheated to which the kitten may escape. Too much heat is as bad as not enough!

Another excellent way to keep kittens warm is to fill one or two small plastic bottles with hot water. Wrap the bottles tightly with towels, and place them in the nest. Such three-dimensional sources of warmth simulate the dam's body and are quickly appreciated by sick kittens. Replenishing hot water every few hours is a bother, but it brings you in contact with your patients frequently and

regularly. Kittens that snuggle to the source of heat indicate they still need the warmth. If all are found away from the warm bottles, you can probably discontinue that support.

If a single kitten is hypothermic, it can be isolated from the others for a few hours while you bring its body temperature up. By confining it to a small space, perhaps a shoe box, it is easier to control and monitor. Keep a thermometer on the source of heat and maintain the temperature of its environment no higher than 100F (37.8°C). Monitor the kitten's body temperature frequently, and when its rectal temperature reaches 97°F (36°C), return it to the dam and watch it closely.

Before a sick, rejected kitten is medicated or fed, take its temperature, stimulate excretions, and clean its anal area. Upon the advice of your veterinarian, feed a milk replacer or dextrose solution warmed to about 97 or 98°F (36 or 37°C) The dextrose solution may be temporarily fed instead of milk replacer if a kitten's body temperature is subnormal, but it shouldn't be used as a maintenance source of nutrition.

The quantity of dextrose or milk replacer that is fed depends upon the condition and age of the kitten. In a newborn, about 2 cc of dextrose or milk replacer should be given every two hours. If the kitten nurses from a bottle, do not limit the quantity of milk replacer fed.

After the necessary treatment and feeding, place the kitten with its

A covered plastic beverage bottle makes an inexpensive kitten-warmer.

mother. If she accepts it, leave it with her until the next treatment. If not, return it to the incubator.

Record Keeping

The importance of day-to-day record keeping can't be over-emphasized. A lot of information can be obtained from your experiences with each litter, and good management is often directly related to good record keeping. Don't rely on your memory! Only accurate, detailed records can be trusted and used in the future. Remember the kittens' individual records that you began when their toenails were painted? Keep those records up-to-date, every day. Those pages should be used to record birth weights, growth weights, appetites, special care, and all other important data. When supplemental feeding is necessary, their formula consumption should be recorded. If illnesses are suspected, the kittens temperatures should be recorded, and if a kitten is particularly weak or aggressive, those notes can be invaluable at a later date.

Complete records are invaluable, even after the kittens are sold. Many conscientious cat breeders continue to follow their queens' progeny until they mature, keeping in touch with new owners, recording show wins and information on the next generation of kittens produced. The more information amassed, the better you can predict the characteristics of future litters from your dam.

Accurate and complete records benefit both breeders and pet owners.

Drug Usage in Neonatal Kittens

The best advice on this subject is to use no drugs without complete specific knowledge of the safety and efficacy of those products. There are a number of reasons for that statement.

- Drug absorption from newborn kittens' gastrointestinal tracts is not identical to that of adult cats.
- Neonates have little muscle mass, and blood supply to their various organs and muscles differ from those of adults.
- Percentage of body fat in neonates is much lower, and fluids are much higher than in adults; thus, drug distribution in newborns is also quite different from adults.
- The protein makeup of kittens differs significantly from adults, and drugs are metabolized at different rates due to kittens' immature enzyme systems.

Tonkinese family.

occur during the first week of life, and half of those are stillbirths.

Birth weights have been proven to be good indicators of the survival potential for kittens. Perhaps the circulatory system maturity accounts for that correlation. Kittens that are born below the normal weight range must be observed more carefully than others.

Other influencing factors that account for some neonatal deaths include environmental temperatures. In addition to the information already provided about queening environment and maternity ward temperatures, you should recognize that neonates do not tolerate sudden temperature changes. They are not physically equipped to handle rapidly increased or decreased environmental temperatures.

Visible birth defects and monstra have also been mentioned, but other, less discernible defects also claim a small toll of neonatal kittens. Internal organ deformities may cause the death of week-old kittens occasionally. Usually kittens with those types of defects will display colic symptoms, anorexia (lack of appetite), or other visible signs.

Obviously, if the dam is suffering from disease or poor nutrition, her kittens are at risk. Sometimes it is necessary to bottle-feed kittens from the day of birth until they begin eating solid food.

Cannibalism is another cause for neonatal deaths. Dams that eat their young usually do so because of crowded, unsanitary, noisy environ-

In short, don't give kittens drugs without specific directions that are applicable to the age and size of the animal to which the drug is being administered. Normal label dosage levels of drugs for adults might be toxic to young kittens, even when calculated on a weight basis.

Neonatal Deaths

After a litter has been successfully brought into the world, good managers concern themselves with maximizing the number of kittens raised to weaning age. In spite of excellent care, all breeding operations will lose an occasional kitten. Published data on kitten losses indicate that average catteries can expect to lose 10 to 30 percent of their full-term neonates. However, I hasten to add that in well-managed catteries, the actual figures are much lower. Most kitten losses

ments. If a queen kills and eats her kittens under normal circumstances, she should be removed from the breeding pool. The propensity to cannibalize may not be a genetically transferred characteristic, but I wouldn't risk breeding such a queen.

Other causes of neonatal deaths include trauma, especially when children are allowed to play with the kittens before they are six weeks old. Infections also account for a few kitten deaths before weaning age.

Orphan Kittens

Before proceeding with this section, go back and read over the section on care of sick kittens (see page 112). Many techniques and precautions apply to both situations.

If you have the misfortune to lose a queen immediately after parturition, don't panic. Kittens are easily reared as orphans. You will spend many hours with the brood during the initial three weeks, but there are personal rewards that compensate you for the time and effort.

If the dam is alive but unable to feed and care for her litter, leave the kittens with her if at all possible. Her physical presence has a positive influence on their personalities. If she is recovering from a serious disease or injury, as soon as she is able, she should have access to her brood. I have seen queens lose their milk production after suffering multiple fractures from some serious

accident. When they are returned to the nursery and see their kittens, they often take up where they left off a week or so previously. They regain milk production, and try very hard to clean and care for their brood.

If the queen has died or is otherwise not available, there are a number of factors to consider as you begin the orphan-rearing chores. The first is a good supply of queen's milk. If the kittens did not receive their mother's colostrum, try to find some. Contact your veterinarian, the officers of feline breed clubs, or all-breed associations. Sometimes, frozen colostrum banks are maintained for just such emergencies.

While searching for colostrum, ask breeders, friends, and veterinarians about potential wet-nurses for the orphan litter. Queens that have delivered small litters of kittens will often adopt a few more to raise as their own. Even if the foster mother's kittens are four or five weeks old, her milk will be superior to commercial,

Six-week-old Devon rex kittens.

artificial formulas. Remember, colostrum production only lasts two or three days, so if an adoptive mother is found, and her litter was born several days previously, you should still try to find a source of colostrum for your orphan brood.

When you find a wet-nurse, introduce the orphans to her very carefully. For the first day or two, place the new kittens with her only while you are present. Once she accepts them and begins to lick and clean them, you can probably trust her not to harm them.

Whether or not colostrum is available, if a foster mother isn't available, ask your pet's doctor to advise you which of the many artificial formulas is best. Don't feed cow's or goat's milk. Buy a canned feline milk formula that has a satisfactory ingredient analysis, and that has been used successfully by others.

While at the pet supply store, purchase three or four of the smallest pet nursing bottles available. Be sure to get the kits that include cleaning brushes and spare nipples. The bottles and nipples should always be cleaned with hot water and soap after every use. They don't need cleaning between kittens under normal circumstances.

Feed the kittens as much formula as they will take, four or five times daily the first two weeks, then three or four times daily the next two weeks. The formula should be refrigerated between feedings, and warmed to the kittens' body temperature before it is fed. As soon as they

begin eating solid food (see Introducing Solid Kitten Food, page 120) drop the formula meals to two per day.

Provide a stable environment for the kittens in a safe, quiet part of the house. I recommend using a fiberglass cat carrier if available. If not, a cardboard box about 16 inches (40.6 cm) square and 12 inches (30.5 cm) tall is sufficient. The floor should be soft, but firm. A towel stretched over a piece of short-nap carpet is ideal. Warm half of the floor of the nursery box by placing a heating pad under that half. The pad should be set at the lowest setting at first. Keep a household thermometer on the towel that covers the heated part of the floor of the nursery box, and check its temperature several times each day. A second thermometer should be located near the ceiling of the nursery box if it is a covered container. If it is an uncovered box, place the second thermometer about a foot above the floor of the nursery. The floor temperature should be held at about 90°F (32°C), and the ambient temperature above the box at about 77°F (25°C).

In addition to stabilizing the environmental temperatures, it is very important to monitor the kittens' body temperatures at least once or twice daily.

As described previously, many breeders prefer using plastic bottles filled with hot water and tightly wrapped with towels to provide three-dimensional sources of warmth for the kittens. These are more trouble than a heating pad, but kittens seem to like to snuggle against them.

Before each feeding, hold each kitten in one hand, upside down. With a damp sponge or washcloth, stroke the kittens' bellies and bottoms. That massaging will stimulate their fecal and urinary excretions. Without massaging, they may fail to eliminate wastes and may develop colic. After each feeding, brush each kitten's coat with a soft sponge or cloth for a minute or two. That grooming action seems to help stimulate napping in the kittens.

The feeding procedure is simple. Put a measured amount of formula into a bottle, squeeze a drop out onto the tip of the nipple, and rub it on the kitten's lips. If the kitten doesn't immediately grasp the nipple, force the nipple between its gums, with the bottle elevated. If necessary, apply a little squeeze to the plastic bottle to force a drop or two of milk on the neonate's tongue. Don't continue to squeeze the bottle! Neonatal deaths are also caused by drowning!

Formula quantities fed by a nursing bottle should not be restricted. It is extremely unlikely that a kitten will overeat when nursing from a bottle. If, however, you are feeding by a stomach tube, always follow instructions carefully. It is quite possible to overload a kitten's tiny stomach when force-feeding. Stomach tube feeding should never be your first feeding choice for orphan kittens. A lack of normal neonatal nursing activities seems to be associated

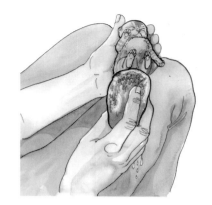

Stimulate an orphan kitten's excretions by massaging its belly with a wet sponge.

with toe sucking and other nuisance behavior of adults. Likewise, if orphan kittens are seen sucking on each other's toes or tails, try to bottle-feed them more frequently.

Provide a soft covering on the floor of the nursery, but don't use loose towels or other bedding that allows an infant to burrow under and become separated from its siblings.

When the orphans are one week old, begin softly massaging their eyelids with cotton balls dampened with ophthalmic boric acid solution or artificial tears. Both of those products are available from the pharmacy. Be particularly careful not to exert pressure on the unopened eyes. A minute of moist massaging three or four times daily is sufficient. When their eyelids begin to separate, continue the moisture applications around the openings, but do not touch the cotton directly to the eyeballs. After their eyes have been open for a day or two, the massaging activity can be discontinued unless an ocular discharge is seen.

119

Introducing Solid Kitten Food

Whether the litter is being raised by their dam or as orphans, about a week after the kittens' eyes have all opened, it is about time to begin solid food introduction. There are many ways to begin feeding cat food, but my favorite is to use a mixture of premium canned kitten food, dry kitten food, and artificial queen's milk. Your success in this endeavor won't be instantaneous, so don't be impatient.

Mix a teaspoonful of the canned food and a like quantity of dry food with enough canned milk formula to reach a consistency of gravy. Warm it to about 85°F (29.4°C) in a saucer. Put the saucer on a layer of newspaper, and set a kitten on the paper facing the food dish. Gently push the kitten's muzzle into the gruel; it will usually begin licking the mixture from its whiskers. Repeat the dunking procedure a few times with each kitten in turn, until all have tasted the food.

Egyptian mau kitten.

Some aggressive eaters will catch on immediately and begin to search for the food on the first exposure. Others will take several sessions before they get the idea. Within three or four days, the litter should be looking forward to their next meal.

As the kittens consume more and more of the solid food, you can begin to gradually change its composition and consistency. First, decrease the amount of formula, allowing the mixture to become less liquid each day. Then, when the kittens are eating softened dry kitten food and canned food, stop mixing the two ingredients, and allow free-choice access to the moistened dry food, supplemented with three meals of canned food each day. When that routine is established, stop moistening the dry food.

If one or more of the kittens are gluttons that dominate feeding time, walk in the saucer, and try to eat everything in sight, it may be necessary to separate the kittens into two or three pairs, keeping each pair isolated from their siblings during feeding times. This is easily accomplished by use of small disposable cardboard boxes.

If the queen is present, another minor and easily controlled problem is sometimes seen. When the very palatable kitten food is introduced to the litter, the dam may wolf the food down as quickly as you are out of sight. If that occurs, place the saucer(s) of food under a creep feeder. Such a device is easily constructed out of an old plastic basket.

Cut a notch out of one or two sides, just large enough for the three-week old kittens to squeeze through. Then turn the basket upside down over the saucers of food. Put a heavy object on the basket to prevent the queen from turning it over, and push the kittens through the notches toward their food. They will soon learn how to enter the creep feeder on their own.

Litter Training

When kittens begin to eat solid food, their mother will stop consuming their excretions. It is, therefore, very important that when you begin supplementing their nursing with solid food, you also place a couple of litter pans in the nursery. Usually, the mother will use the pans first, and the kittens will copy their mother and begin to use them almost immediately. It is important to furnish one litter box for each two cats. Even tiny kittens appreciate clean, fresh litter.

If the kittens don't catch on to litter box use quickly, you can help teach them. When you clean up their excretions, place some of the feces in each box, covered with a thin layer of litter. Then pick up each kitten in turn and place it in the box. Repeat the procedure several times daily and they will soon be using the litter exclusively.

Chapter 13
Weaning Kittens

After her kittens are eating solid food, the mother will instinctively pay less attention to her brood, and she may voluntarily stop nursing them. If she continues to be possessive of her babies and shows no desire to wean them, let her instincts rule. You should never forcibly separate kittens from their dam before they are at least eight to ten weeks old. If she voluntarily stops feeding them before that time, leave the family together anyway. Her influence goes far beyond her feeding activities. Orphan kittens are often sold too early. If possible, leave the litter together until they are two months old.

Emotional Maturity

When are kittens ready to be weaned and sent into new homes? Much depends on each individual kitten's physical and personality development. All kittens of a litter don't necessarily mature at the same rate. It is dangerous and inadvisable to set a pre-selected age at which an entire litter is ready for new homes. Instead, watch each kitten's interaction with its siblings, its mother, and its human family. When a kitten begins to venture away from its dam to investigate the world outside the nursery, it is approaching the age for leaving the nest. You might observe maturing kittens contentedly snoozing in a corner by themselves, instead of in a pile against their mother.

When a kitten begins to play independently with its siblings, hiding behind objects and attacking its brothers or sisters, separation age is close. Emotional maturity is also indicated when a kitten immediately begins to

Blue Somali cat.

play with a toy on a string, and doesn't require coaxing to leave the nest or when it doesn't fidget and struggle when you pick it up for a cuddle.

The final test is passed when a kitten leaves the nest to come to you when you approach, expecting a play period, cuddling, or grooming. In some, that age might be as early as seven weeks of age; in others it might be ten or twelve weeks. Don't be in a hurry! Kittens that are shy or reclusive should be kept in their nursery environment until they become socialized and relatively independent.

Socialization and Bonding

Human socialization should begin shortly after the kittens' eyes open. By three or four weeks of age, they should be accustomed to being individually handled by adult humans. During the third to twelfth weeks of a kitten's life, human companionship can be indelibly imprinted on their developing personalities. Gently petting and cuddling kittens when they are three or four weeks old is as important as playing with them with a ball on a string when they are six or seven weeks old. In both cases, the impressionable and dependent feline is positively influenced by loving humans.

The human-cat bond will form quickly and last a lifetime when it is carefully engineered at an early age. That is not meant to imply that such bonding can't occur when the kittens are older; it just requires more time and patience. The early bonding is easily transferred to a new owner, when that person displays similar love and attention to the kitten.

Remember that negative acts will be just as deeply imprinted as positive ones. Take great care that the kittens are not frightened, injured, or abused during that impressionable period. Children should handle the kittens only when well supervised by adults.

Weaning Preparations and Diet

Sometimes individual kittens are physically separated from the nest as they are sold, but in other instances, it may be advisable to wean them as a litter. This is often the case when a breeder wishes to keep the kittens for a few weeks to watch color changes or coat pattern development. Many times, it is impossible to choose the best kittens to keep in a cattery's breeding program until they are three or four months old.

When a litter of kittens are separated from their dam, give them free access to a premium dry kitten food and at least two meals of premium canned kitten food each day. At least one bowl of water should be available and replenished daily. Supply the brood with a scratching post, clip their toenails, and provide at

Creep-feeding prevents the dam from eating the kittens' food.

least one litter pan for every two or three kittens. An easily cleaned bathroom or a large cat kennel makes an excellent weaning nursery.

When individuals are separated from the litter and sold one by one, it is very important that the new owners understand what is being fed, how often, and about how much. Never leave such important facts undocumented. Probably the greatest error made by new kitten owners is dietary mismanagement. I have treated hundreds of newly acquired kittens for digestive disorders and dehydration, all because the new owner assumed that the best food for the eight-week-old kitten was all the milk it could drink.

Examination for Congenital Defects

At approximately weaning age, and before they are offered for sale, the kittens should be examined by your veterinarian to verify their good health and freedom from congenital abnormalities. If you keep the kittens until eight or nine weeks of age, they can receive their first vaccination on the same visit. When vaccinated, ask the veterinarian to prepare a vaccination record for each kitten. It should include the brand name, type of vaccine used, and date given. On the same record, or independently, a record of other physical examinations should be noted. If possible, have the litter examined in your home, rather than taking them to an animal hospital.

A composite sample of the litter's feces should be taken to your veterinarian at this time also, to diagnose and prescribe treatment for any existing parasite problem.

Your veterinarian's statement of health for each kitten should be a complete record that clearly identifies the kitten by sex, color, and markings. It should list all problems diagnosed, their treatment, and the results of the fecal examination. That record, in addition to its vaccination history, weight record, date of solid food introduction, and weaning date, should accompany the kitten to its new home.

Selling Kittens

Sooner or later, the time comes to start thinking about sharing the joy of feline ownership with the cat-loving community. There are several items of business that must be attended to before offering your kittens to the public.

A three-generation pedigree should be included in the kitten's documents. (Pedigrees and registration procedures are discussed in Chapter 15). When the kittens join their new owners, a kitten registration form should accompany each one, unless other arrangements are made. For instance, if you place a mismarked kitten in a home as a pet, you might agree with the buyer ahead of time that it is to be neutered and not allowed to reproduce. In that case, you might also agree to retain its registration papers until the buyer furnishes proof of neutering.

Give specific dietary advice to the buyers of your kittens. I recommend providing the buyer with written feeding instructions together with a bag and several cans of the food being used. Impress upon the new owner the importance of keeping the diet stable, without any supplements or additives, for at least a month.

Try to remember all the questions that you asked when you acquired your purebred kitten, and be prepared to answer them. You have now assumed the role of cat breeder, and novices will pick your brain before making their selection from your brood.

Be sure to observe the litter carefully to assure that all are eating well and are playful and active. If you suspect that a kitten's appetite is not equal to others, separate them at

Kittens show signs of independence at about six weeks.

feeding time for a day or two. Feed each kitten a couple of teaspoonsful of canned food, in separate bowls, in different rooms or parts of the house.

Evaluate the quality of each kitten before prospective buyers are invited to see your brood. Although the kittens have the same genetic makeup, they will differ in value according to their conformity to the breed standard. In this regard, it is sometimes best to secure the opinion of an unbiased third party. Another breeder friend or an associate you have met at a cat show will suffice. Perhaps you know a judge who might help.

Contacting Prospective Buyers

If you have been showing the dam, selling the best of her offspring should present no great problem. Word of mouth or a note in your breed club's

newsletter will bring inquiries from interested breeders. Purebred kittens of lesser quality deserve good homes, too. A mismarked body or less than desirable conformation is no reason to hide a kitten in the closet. Most all kittens make great pets, even if they can't win show titles.

Pets can be advertised in various media, including magazines, newsletters, and newspapers. To avoid misunderstandings, be sure your advertisements identify the quality of kittens being offered. When you receive phone call inquiries, make your sale policy known to the caller. If you require that the pet be altered at maturity, or if you plan to withhold pedigree and registration until proof of altering is shown, let the prospective buyer know those restrictions up front. If prices are negotiable, give potential owners your starting figure and let them know that you might consider a counteroffer.

Early Spaying or Castration

Although the procedure is not yet in common use, kittens and puppies have recently been spayed or castrated at very young ages, before weaning. The results of these carefully controlled tests are very encouraging. Few complications have been noted; growth patterns and personality development seem to be nearly normal. Risks are quite small, and the practice is already beginning to take hold in a few animal shelters across the United States. I believe that early neutering of pet-quality kittens may be a viable option for conscientious cat breeders in the future. I encourage you to ask your veterinarian about the procedure, and consider it for kittens with features that are less than desirable. A certain number of pet-quality kittens seem to crop up in every litter. Neutering those pets before they leave the breeders' catteries might be instrumental in establishing and maintaining more uniform breeding stock in every breed. I believe it might be a way for professional breeders to better control the gene pool of their particular breeds.

Meeting Prospective Owners

Purebred cat breeders have an extended obligation when they sell a kitten. You must back your kittens with certain guarantees. Discuss that subject with other breeders, read breed club newsletter articles, or write for advice from established breeders. You will probably find that most ethical purebred cat breeders will take back any cat they sell if the buyer can no longer care for it. Some may even refund a portion of the purchase price.

When potential kitten buyers telephone, screen them discreetly. Keeping your inquiries circumspect, try to discover as much as you can about other pets in their home, how much space is available, how the kitten will be housed, the buyers' reasons for

wanting a cat, and their desire and capability to care for the kitten.

If they plan to visit your home or cattery to see your litter, ask them not to handle other cats immediately before coming. Explain that certain diseases can be transmitted by human vectors. When they arrive, if they have been handling other kittens, provide soap and water and a clean towel. If they understand your motives, they will wash their hands and appreciate your concern.

Ask the buyers to watch the kittens from a distance first. Take them to the nursery, or bring the kittens out where they can be observed. If possible, sit down with the prospective new owners and let the kittens play on the floor. Have some toys ready, and be sure there is a litter box in sight. It is a serious mistake to bring the kittens out one by one, handing them to the buyer. When a

A curious Bengal kitten.

kitten is abruptly taken from the nursery and given to a stranger, it will probably be frightened and will hide the moment it is released.

Be sure to mention the nail polish identification code on the kittens' rear toenails. That becomes very important when several kittens have the same color and patterns.

Prospective owners appreciate knowing what the kitten will look like as an adult. Have the dam present, and if the sire is not immediately available, his picture will help. If you own cats from the dam's previous litters, parade them also. Be sure to identify any kittens in the litter that are not for sale.

Show them the pedigree and registration papers of the litter, as well as any contracts or agreements that apply to the sale. Let them see the health and vaccination records, including the need for booster vaccinations. Discuss the show and breeding potential of the various kittens offered for sale.

It is very important that prospective buyers understand the cat overpopulation problem. If they are searching for a pet instead of a breeding animal, impress upon them the need for castration or spaying at the appropriate time. An agreement or contract may be used to further promote altering pets. Inform them of the hazards of allowing their pet outside, whether altered or not.

Chapter 14
Health Care

The health of your cat depends upon many factors, including proper immunization. To vaccinate a kitten and provide it with food and water does not assure its good health. The health or disease status of a cat is the product of physical, emotional, infectious, and nutritional factors. Those factors are interrelated and include the animal's genetic makeup, exposure to diseases, the population density of the environment (the number of cats in the household or cattery), the quality and quantity of nutrition provided, exercise provisions, sanitation of the physical environment, and both natural and induced disease immunity. Cats are emotionally somewhat like humans; those that are loved and petted regularly are usually happy and contented.

Rumors or grapevine networks may suggest that mixed-breed cats enjoy more disease resistance and live longer, healthier lives than purebreds. Perhaps it is true that a hybrid vigor factor may exist in kittens that are the product of a dam and sire that have distinctly different genetic makeups. Often, I believe, that factor is overstated. I have dis-

covered apparent genetic weaknesses in farm or ranch cat communities, probably associated with the long breeding life of a particularly dominant tom. Those cats are surely not purebreds, yet by line breeding or inbreeding, recessive genetic faults eventually surface.

By the same measure, purebred cats that are produced by careful selection may possess vigor similar to that of mixed breeds. Breeding programs should always consider the health of the dam, sire, and every kitten produced. When weak kittens, stillbirths, or fading kittens occur, your breeding program should be reevaluated.

Sphynx. Who said we looked like mice?

Vaccination Schedules

Kitten vaccinations for various diseases are important to maintain your cat's good health, and the rapidly developing field of biotechnology introduces new immunizing agents annually. Diseases may be endemic in some parts of the country, and totally absent in others. It is not my intent to furnish a biologic product inventory, or to advise you which vaccine to use at certain ages. Any arbitrary vaccination schedule is worthless unless it addresses new products and your geographical location. The following discussion will instead give you as much health and immunization information as possible. Your cat's specific vaccination schedule should originate with your local veterinarian.

What Is a Vaccine?

Vaccines are biologic agents that when properly administered to a healthy animal, cause that animal to develop immunity to a disease. Some vaccines are prepared from killed bacteria, viruses, or other microscopic pathogens (disease-causing organisms). Those killed products are usually considered to be safer to use, especially in very young and very old animals. They are probably inferior to the live vaccines in terms of protection because they do not replicate in the vaccinated animal's tissues and the immune response is slower and less complete.

Other vaccines are made from living microscopic pathogenic organisms (primarily viruses), which have been treated in some way to modify or attenuate them. Modification allows the infectious agent to remain alive, but prevents it from causing disease. When such an agent is introduced into a healthy animal, it replicates in the tissues of that animal, causing no actual disease but stimulating antibody response. Those are modified live-virus (MLV) vaccines, and they are generally believed to confer more reliable immunity than killed-virus vaccines. Replicating vaccine viruses may be shed from the vaccinated animals.

Recent technical advances involve the preparation of vaccines from particles of viruses. Fragments of a virus are split away from the disease-causing organism. When administered to a healthy animal, they stimulate an immune response in the vaccinated animal, but it is impossible for the fragments to cause disease.

How a Vaccine Works

Vaccines may be administered by intramuscular or subcutaneous injections, or in some cases, by aerosol mist or drops placed into the nasal openings or conjunctival sac between the eyelids. Vaccines are intended to stimulate a dynamic, ongoing process called *immune response*. That biological response involves the production of white blood cells and antibodies that independently attack and destroy invading pathogens before they can cause disease. Immune response includes the establishment of a memory process (*anamnesis*) that hastens future responses to exposures to the infectious agent.

The level of immunity that develops from a vaccination is dependent upon the cat's health, its age, its existing passive immunity, its prior vaccination history, and its past exposure to the pathogen. The degree or quality of immunity conferred by a vaccine is also related to the particular infectious agent involved, its antigenicity, the vaccine concentration, and the route of vaccine administration. When a cat has some degree of immunity to a disease, and is subsequently vaccinated for that disease, its immunity will normally be boosted. Without booster vaccinations or exposure to disease-causing organisms, the cat's immunity gradually decreases. It is important that booster vaccinations are given regularly to stimulate and maintain the anamnestic (memory) response in a vaccinated animal. Vaccines are not perfect.

A strong, healthy cat in top nutritional condition will resist disease by virtue of its good health. A healthy cat will also respond well to vaccinations and will develop more complete immunity to diseases. Vaccinations given to cats suffering from poor nutrition, disease, or other stresses may be a waste of biologics and can give owners a false sense of security.

Vaccines aren't treatments for existing diseases. They are worth-

Bengals. Who's too big to nurse?

less, and may even be contraindicated, once a disease process has begun. A preventive medicine program is important in any cat breeding operation, and vaccinations must be an integral part of that program.

Vaccination Safety

Some cat breeders believe that only killed-virus vaccines should be used in kittens, because the safety and effectiveness of modified live-virus (MLV) vaccines aren't proven in youngsters. There is a potential (if remote) threat that a virus contained in an MLV vaccine might revert to a disease-causing state. In my conversations with representatives from the leading vaccine manufacturers, I have found no documentation indicating that any of the current MLV viruses have ever reverted to a virulent state and caused a disease in domestic felines.

Virus shedding may occur when certain MLV vaccines are administered. The shedding is related to the fact that an MLV virus replicates in the tissues of the vaccinated animal. Shed viruses aren't necessarily *virulent* (capable of causing disease).

There are reports of virus shedding from vaccinated domestic cats causing symptoms in wild feline species that are housed near the vaccinated domestic cats. If you keep exotic feline species in your home, your vaccination program should be discussed with veterinarians who have experience with vaccines used in those animals. Many veterinarians who specialize in wild-feline medicine use killed-vaccines in exotic cats such as the lynx and Asian leopard cats.

Any individual cat may suffer an adverse reaction to a drug or vaccine. That is a calculated risk taken by veterinarians and cat owners every day. In my experience, there is no significant risk associated with vaccinations of healthy cats by professionals who have experience with the products being administered.

Infectious Diseases with Available Vaccines

Rabies is a fatal disease of all mammals. In nature, it is transmitted by direct contact with the saliva of infected animals. It is, therefore, rarely a threat to confined house cats, and another good reason to keep your feline friends confined to your home. Feline rabies vaccina-

tion requirements vary from place to place according to local ordinances. Vaccination is required by at least 12 states' statutes. Whether required or not, I believe cats should be vaccinated against rabies. Consult with your veterinarian at about what age your cat should be vaccinated, as well as the need for booster vaccinations.

The most common reservoirs of infection for rabies virus are raccoons, bats, skunks, and other wild mammals. All rabies vaccines currently in use are killed-virus products.

Healthy cats may be vaccinated initially between three and six months of age, then again when one year old. A booster may be given every one to three years, depending upon the particular vaccine used and applicable laws.

Feline leukemia virus (FeLV) causes a complex, often fatal disease in cats that may be manifested in many different ways. It may suppress the cat's immune system and cause severe anemia, and it is frequently associated with cancer of the lymph glands, bones, nerves, lungs, gastrointestinal tracts, and kidneys. Often, the only outwardly visible symptoms are gradual health degeneration, weight loss, lethargy, and depression.

FeLV can be contracted through bite wounds and other physical contacts with infected animals, or it can be transmitted from mother to kittens before or at the time of birth. Blood tests can detect FeLV, but the interpretation and significance of test results are controversial in the veterinary community at this time. FeLV tests and vaccination programs vary from one area of the country to another, and from year to year, as new research results are published and new biologics are developed. Because FeLV is so unpredictable, your cat's doctor should be consulted before testing or vaccinating.

Feline acquired immune deficiency syndrome (FAIDS) is a condition that seems to be induced by FeLV. It is manifested by a general reduction of the functional immune system of an infected animal. Cats with immune deficiencies are susceptible to virtually dozens of infectious agents. The syndrome has been associated with cases of feline infectious peritonitis (FIP), chronic respiratory infections, recurrent abscesses, and many others. According to current knowledge, the condition is not transmissible to other species.

Feline panleukopenia virus (FPV) (cat distemper or feline enteritis) is one of the most common and severe viral diseases of cats. It is especially lethal in young kittens, but it can cause death at any age. In very young kittens, the disease is often overwhelming; a kitten may appear normal one moment and become lethargic and limp a few hours later. Within a few more hours, the infected kitten may be comatose or even dead. In older cats, the symptoms usually include severe diarrhea, vomiting, and dehydration.

Birman cleaning itself.

Panleukopenia is especially relevant in a feline breeding program. The virus quickly invades the uterus of a pregnant female, crosses the placental barrier, and invades fetuses. It then infects the central nervous systems, causing abortion, stillbirths, or brain defects and monstra.

A series of vaccinations against panleukopenia is recommended for all kittens, beginning by eight to ten weeks of age, depending on the circumstances. Annual booster vaccinations are essential.

Feline viral rhinotracheitis (FVR) is one of several feline upper respiratory diseases. It is typically manifested by sneezing, purulent ocular and nasal discharge, and redness of the membranes of the eyes. Cats affected with that disease often dehydrate rapidly, and frequently they have no appetite. Those complications make the disease noteworthy in all ages, but especially in the young. Rhinotracheitis may be accompanied by pneumonia, which can be fatal.

Although FVR is usually associated with respiratory symptoms, it is another cause for feline abortions and possibly fetal resorption when unprotected pregnant cats are exposed.

"Rhino" is usually spread by aerosol (sneeze) contact from infected cats. It is most prevalent in outdoor cats or in animals that are exposed to infected cats in boarding kennels or cat shows. House cats can contract the disease from infected stray cats through open, screened windows or doors. A fairly common symptom of FVR is tongue lesions. They appear as deep, red ulcers on the surface of infected animals' tongues. These lesions are painful and contribute to the *anorexia* (loss of appetite) that typifies the disease.

Vaccination is recommended for all cats. The vaccine is often packaged in combination with other vaccines.

Calicivirus (FHV-1) complex usually always causes erosions on the tongue, lips, gums, nostrils, throat, and sometimes the inner mucous membranes of the eyelids. It is often complicated by a reduced appetite and dehydration. This disease usually runs a relatively short course, and is rarely fatal, but if untreated, the appetite loss and dehydration problems can be very serious. As in other viral diseases, infection with calicivirus reduces the animal's resistance to other diseases. It is often diagnosed concurrently with rhinotracheitis, and is also spread by aerosol.

Vaccinations are recommended for all cats, using the same schedule as FVR and FPV vaccinations.

Chlamydiosis (pneumonitis) is a disease that is manifested by sneezing and inflammation of the membranes of the nostrils and the eyes. It is caused by the Chlamydia organism that is neither a virus nor a bacterium. The infection produces symptoms similar to calici and rhinotracheitis viruses. It is highly contagious and may occur in cattery situations as a neonatal disease. It is treatable with antibiotics, and is, thus, less dangerous than calici or rhinotracheitis. Unfortunately, all three of these diseases may infect a cat concurrently.

Chlamydia vaccine is a killed product that is frequently combined with the vaccines for panleukopenia, calici, and rhinotracheitis. The same vaccination schedule may be used.

Vaccines for the upper respiratory diseases discussed above are usually protective; however they are not 100 percent effective under all circumstances. Booster vaccinations are very important. Remember,

in order to be effective, vaccinations must be given before the kitten or cat is exposed to the diseases.

Feline infectious peritonitis (FIP) is caused by a coronavirus and is a lethal viral disease of cats. In the early stages, symptoms of the disease include a persistent fever, but other signs are very obscure. Later, infected cats may suffer from abdominal or chest fluid production. There is no known successful treatment for the disease. It does not occur as frequently as the other feline diseases discussed, and is not as well understood as most other cat diseases.

A vaccine is available, but veterinarians often recommend FIP vaccination only in high-risk situations.

Hemobartonellosis is an infectious disease of cats that causes anemia, depression, and loss of appetite. It is contagious, but no vaccine is presently available. The disease is caused by a bacterium, *Hemobartonella felis,* that attaches to and parasitizes the red blood cells of affected cats, destroying those cells. Early in the course of the infection, the cats run fevers of 104 to 105°F (40–40.6°C). Later, anemia is seen, resulting in weakness, pale mucous membranes, and loss of weight. Sometimes red blood cell destruction is sufficiently extensive to cause jaundice, or yellow discoloration of the cats' mucous membranes.

Ear mites are frequently associated with otitis externa. This extremely common condition is caused by a transmissible parasitic mite, *Otodectes cyanotis.* These tiny

135

white mites can be seen with magnifying glasses. They reside deep in cats' ear canals, causing irritation and itching. A presumptive diagnosis is often based on a large amount of black or dark brown wax and obvious ear discomfort. Cats with ear mite infestations display the signs of otitis discussed above.

An additional significance of mite infestations is their transmission from cat to cat, and it is rare to see the condition in only one cat of a multi-cat household. Treatment consists of thorough ear cleaning, and medicating the ear canals daily with specific mite-killing drops. I have always cautioned owners to put a drop of mite medication on the tips of infested cats' tails at the same time the ears were treated. I have repeatedly found live ear mites on the tail hair. I suspect the mites

Somali kittens. Try to choose just one!

vacated their natural habitat when washing and treatment began, crawling out of the canals onto the closest structure, which is usually the tail tip. Then, when the all-clear whistle is sounded, they migrate back into the ears, confounding both owners and veterinarians.

Ear mites may also be found causing itching, scabby lesions on cats' forepaws and cheeks. Again, I wonder if those infestations aren't begun by mites escaping from ear canal therapy. When ear mites are diagnosed, most veterinarians will treat all cats of the household, and will often prescribe the use of a feline-safe insecticide powder to be applied to other parts of the cats' bodies.

Noncontagious Diseases

Feline urological syndrome (FUS or **FLUTD)** is in a class by itself, and it claims the lives of thousands of adult male cats annually. In contemporary literature, the syndrome is called feline lower urinary tract disease (FLUTD). Until the advent of new, carefully balanced commercial diets for cats, FLUTD was one of the most common, potentially fatal disease syndromes seen in male cats.

FLUTD refers to a blockage of the urethra of male cats. It is caused by mucus plugs and tiny sandlike stones (struvite crystals) that originate in the urinary bladder. Within hours after total urethral obstruction, the cat begins to suffer intense abdominal pain, and if not treated very early, the cat will absorb toxic waste products from his urine. In the absence of treatment, kidney degeneration and uremic poisoning follow and the cat will die.

The mucus plugs and crystal formation probably occur in many female cats as well, but due to the anatomical differences between the male and female, only the male's life is frequently at risk. A male cat's urethra bends around the pelvic bone, then it narrows as it passes through the penis (see illustration, page 53). Solid and semisolid particles collect in that curved funnel, and obstructions are formed. The shorter, wider, more elastic urethra of the female allows mucus and crystals to pass without obstructing urine flow.

FLUTD is a medical emergency! If symptoms are observed, your veterinarian should be called immediately.

Initially, an affected cat makes frequent trips to his litter pan. He strains for a few seconds, then leaves the pan, only to return a short while later and repeat the process. He licks his penis and perineal area frequently. When you check the litter to see if any urine has been passed, you may see none, or perhaps only a few drops, often accompanied by a drop or two of blood.

As the condition progresses, he squats in the litter box in a urinating or defecating position for extended periods of time, and often cries in pain. By that time, he will be totally disinterested in food and water.

Goin' for a buggy ride.

Later, he will appear disoriented and glassy eyed. He will lie on his side and cry in pain when touched.

Cats sometimes give their owners early warning signs of urinary disease. They will jump into a sink, bathtub, or shower, or onto a countertop or table, and urinate on those obvious locations. Often the urine will contain a few drops of blood mixed with the urine. If your cat sends those messages to you, take it to your veterinarian before other symptoms develop.

FLUTD is seen in all breeds of cats in all parts of the country. It is not as common today as it was in the past, but if it should occur, your male cat's life may depend upon early detection of FLUTD symptoms and immediate veterinary treatment.

Hair ball (trichobezoar) formation in the stomach and intestines of cats is a common condition. As cats groom themselves, they swallow hair that is pulled out with their raspy tongues. Hair is nearly indigestible, and it mats into tightly woven masses in their stomachs or upper small intestines. Those indigestible hair masses must be passed through the cats' bowels, or be vomited. Cats with hair balls may exhibit persistent dry coughs and reduced appetites shortly before vomiting a mouse-shaped hair ball. Treatment, if required, usually employs the regular use of lubricants that may be added to the cats' food, or given directly from a squeeze tube.

Gingivitis is an inflammation or infection of the gums. It is usually associated with dental problems such as heavy tartar on your cats' teeth. The signs usually observed include bad breath and reluctance to pick up or chew solid food. It is a condition seen primarily in middle-age or older cats. Treatment is usually begun by cleaning the teeth and removing the tartar. In advanced cases, a tooth or several teeth may require extraction.

Otitis externa refers to inflammation of the cat's outer ear canals. Affected animals usually scratch at their ears and hold them tipped downward. You may observe a foul-smelling discharge draining from the ears. The inflammation may be caused by an uncomplicated bacter-ial infection, or it may be stimulated by foreign material such as grass seeds that have migrated deep into the ear canals. In my experience, otitis externa cases were frequently caused by ticks that had set up residence deep in the canals, or they were related to an infestation of ear mites (which are contagious). In any case, excessive wax is secreted by the ear canal glands. The waxy buildup in the ear canals causes reduced air flow and provides an excellent incubator for bacteria.

Treatment usually includes thorough cleaning of the ear canals, removal of ticks or foreign material, and home therapy that may include the use of drops in the ear, oral antibiotics, or combinations thereof.

Wounds and abscesses are common in outdoor cats, especially in toms. Abscesses are usually the result of cat fight puncture wounds that are not treated immediately or adequately. Treatment of wounds or abscesses depends upon the location and state of the infection. Prevention is easier, cheaper, and safer than treatment!

Anal sac impactions are nuisance conditions that often worry owners. Scent sacs are normal anatomical structures in many carnivores, including cats and dogs, but they are best developed in skunks. Normally, the foul-smelling scent oil is periodically eliminated from the anal sacs when the cat passes its feces. When the natural opening of an anal sac becomes obstructed with hair, feces, or other solid matter, the oily secretion is trapped within the sac, and the cat suffers some discomfort. Signs of feline anal sac impactions sometimes include scooting on its bottom (which is the most common symptom in dogs). A cat may also display quite different symptoms. It may jump from a resting position, look behind itself as if bitten on the derriere, and often switch its tail violently. Sometimes its skin will twitch or "crawl" from the root of the tail forward along its spine. It may suddenly sit down, turn, and begin licking at its anal area.

When such symptoms are seen, call your veterinarian for an appointment. Impactions are not emergencies, but they should be treated. If the condition occurs frequently, you may want the doctor to teach you how to express the anal sacs at home.

Mammary tumors are most common in middle-age or older cats. They are usually always malignant, requiring surgical mastectomies. They may be found by observant owners when no larger than match heads, but are usually presented to veterinarians when the tumors have become much larger. The earlier they are treated, the less surgical trauma and stress is experienced by the affected queen. They may be located in one or several mammary glands.

The tumors seem to be directly associated with the queen's reproductive cycles, and most veterinarians will advise spaying the patient at the time mastectomies are done.

Skin Diseases

Ringworm is a contagious fungal skin disease of cats. It is more commonly seen in cats that are under stress from overcrowding, lack of exercise, poor nutrition, or an unclean environment. In an acute clinical infection, skin lesions are raised, inflamed, hairless circles on the skin. Subclinical ringworm is much more common, and is manifested by scaling of the skin, broken hair shafts, and only slight hair loss.

Animals with subclinical infections may go unnoticed by owners, and they often act as carriers or reservoirs of infection for other cats, other household pets, and sometimes humans. Fungus infections can be transmitted by handling an infected animal, then handling a susceptible animal.

Specific diagnosis is not always easy, and must be made in a clinical

The flea is a common source for tapeworm infestation.

139

laboratory. Treatment varies according to the circumstances. It may be necessary to use oral medication, topical medication, medicated baths, or a combination of techniques.

Mange is a less commonly diagnosed skin disease of cats. It may be caused by any of several skin mites including *Demodex,* the *Notoedric* mite, or *Cheyletiella.*

Diagnosis is made in the laboratory and treatment is managed by specific drugs applied to the skin. Mange is often related to stress factors, and some veterinarians recommend vitamin therapy and nutritional improvement in addition to specific therapeutic products.

Flea bites can cause small irritating, oozing skin lesions. More significant is an allergy that causes intense itching, especially in the areas of the base of the tail and along the flanks. The cause of the intense skin inflammation is an allergic reaction to the fleas' saliva. In extensive flea infestations, sufficient blood may be sucked from the hosts to cause anemia. Probably the most dramatic result of flea bites is the grouchy

Russian blue kittens.

attitude of an infested cat. Obviously, the diagnosis depends upon finding fleas or the excreta of fleas on the cat, and definitive treatment is aimed toward ridding the cat of the flea infestation.

Dietary hypersensitivity is not common, but it is occasionally seen in all animals. The symptoms are generalized pruritus (itching), over most of the body. After ruling out more common causes of skin irritation, diet changes may be prescribed to ascertain which ingredient in the cat's diet is causing the problem. Fortunately, there are now foods available that make both diagnosis and treatment of allergies easier.

Lick ulcers are among the most frustrating conditions to treat. Often called *rodent ulcers* or *lick granulomas,* I found them most commonly on the upper lips of affected cats. They may occur on other parts of the body, including the feet and foreleg skin. They can become very unsightly scarlike lesions that seem to resist all therapy efforts.

I doubt if anyone understands the cause for these terrible skin ulcers. I believe some are due to minor trauma of the lip, followed by habitual, nearly continual, licking of the traumatized tissue. The cat's spiny tongue seems to perpetuate the original traumatic lesion, and, with time, red, firm scar tissue builds on the area. Researchers have suggested bacterial infections and allergies as other possible causes. I know of cats that have had their canine teeth extracted because they were assumed to be the cause of irritation that stimulated the ulcer formation.

Lick ulcers on the lips are most frequently treated with cortisone-like drugs, administered orally or by injection. Topical treatments are usually not effective and will more likely increase the cat's licking, thereby resulting in exacerbation of the lesions. In neutered males and spayed females, progesterone products have also been used successfully in some cases. In my practice, I have tried electrocautery, but found *cryosurgery* (freezing with liquid nitrogen) to be somewhat more reliable in removing the inflamed masses.

When the ulcers occur on feet and legs, restricting the cat's access to those areas is essential. Bandaging or the use of Elizabethan collars to stop licking improves the chances that therapy will be successful. Many cases that aren't treated early do not respond to any therapy.

Feline acne is another sometimes recurring condition that offers a challenge to both the owner and the veterinarian. The condition is not the same as acne seen in humans. In the cat, it involves the hair follicles and large oil glands of the skin covering the cat's chin.

The lesions initially appear like little blackheads that are tender to touch. A pathogenic bacteria can sometimes be cultured from the pustules that form deep to the blackheads. Affected cats scratch at the lesions, and some animals run low-grade fevers and become depressed. The tenderness of the

If allowed to progress, feline acne can become a serious, difficult disease to treat.

chin seems to inhibit eating to a degree in some pets.

Mild cases will respond to shaving the area and gentle washing of the lesions two or three times daily. Mild povidone iodine soaps are sometimes effective, if used frequently. Veterinarians may prescribe benzoyl peroxide products to apply after the area is cleaned with soap and water. If the pustules enlarge and become abscesses, they may require surgical drainage. A few acne pustules coalesce and develop into a network of tunnels under the skin, all of which are infected. General anesthesia is often required to allow for thorough cleaning, draining, and flushing of such advanced acne lesions. Systemic antibiotics are often given for a week or two to help control the bacterial infections associated with acne.

Contact dermatitis, caused by chemical irritants, is seen when cats get too close to fresh paint, tar, turpentine, solvents, or a host of other common household chemicals. Another chemical that may cause contact dermatitis is the insecticide used in the manufacture of flea collars. I found the condition most frequently in cats that were fitted with flea and tick collars that were too small. When the insecticide-impregnated plastic collars remain in constant, tight contact with a cat's skin, an irritation may result.

Contact dermatitis is recognized by inflammation of the skin at the point of contact with the chemical agent. Sometimes the outer layers of the skin slough, leaving scabby, oozing lesions. Treatment is usually directed at removing the irritant, washing thoroughly, and applying mild, soothing topical creams or ointments. Sometimes, cortisone-like drugs are given orally or by injection or applied topically to reduce the inflammation.

Devon rex kittens. Where's my coat?

Internal Parasites

There are a number of internal parasites that may infest your cats. Some of those parasites can be passed from a queen to her kittens at birth or shortly thereafter. Infestations may be the result of exposure to parasite eggs (or larvae) that are shed from other infested cats as well. Not all worms or other internal parasites are large enough to be seen with the naked eye, and diagnosis is made in a laboratory.

Tapeworms are two-host parasites often infesting cats that kill and eat certain small rodents, or in those that are infested with fleas. Either fleas or rodents may be secondary hosts for tapeworm larvae. If a cat ingests infested fleas or rodents, tapeworm adults will develop in the intestine of the cat (see illustration, page 143). Tapeworm adults are segmented, thin, flat parasites that grow to great lengths in the cat's intestinal tract. As the worms mature, small segments drop off and may be found in the infested cat's feces or stuck to the hair around its anus. Dried tapeworm segments look like tiny grains of rice, and finding those segments on your cat is diagnostic for tapeworms.

Roundworms, especially the nematode *Toxocara cati,* have a complex life cycle in cats. They are known to infest kittens at an early age through the infested mother's milk. Skinny, inactive kittens should be suspected of infestation. Breeding queens should have a fecal examination done before they are bred, to assure that they are not infested.

Ancylostoma (hookworm) infestations are rare in the United States, but when they occur, they are quite significant because they may cause intestinal bleeding. Thin, inactive, weak, or anemic-appearing kittens might be suspected of harboring hookworms.

Toxoplasma infestation is rare, but that protozoan parasite has public health significance and should be discussed with your veterinarian, whether or not it is suspected in your cat.

Isospora are coccidia that are relatively common in cats. Coccidiosis may cause chronic diarrhea and weight loss in the hosts, and the parasite more frequently infests outdoor cats.

Diagnosis of the above and other internal parasites is usually made through microscopic examinations of the feces of your pet. A fresh fecal sample from your breeding stock and kittens should be taken to your veterinarian for laboratory examination at least once a year.

Hormonal Imbalances

Hyperthyroidism is a hormonal imbalance that is occasionally seen in middle-age and older cats. Its external symptoms include weight loss, increased appetite accompanied by voluminous stool produc-

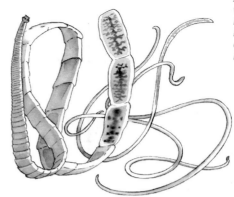

Adult tapeworms and roundworms live in the cat's small intestines.

tion, restlessness, excitability, and increased shedding. It is diagnosed by physical examination and laboratory blood tests.

Hypothyroidism, the near opposite to the above condition, is also most frequently seen in older cats. It is believed to be a familial disease, and is occasionally diagnosed in young kittens as well. It is a disorder that might be suspected in older cats that are obese, poorly groomed, soft, and lethargic. Most cats with thyroid insufficiency have a slow pulse and seek warmth. Like hyperthyroidism, blood tests may help to identify the disease, but more commonly it is diagnosed by the cat's response to a course of treatment based on the doctor's previous experience with cats having similar symptoms.

Hyperadrenocortism is another uncommon hormonal disease that sometimes accompanies or mimics diabetes. The outward symptoms

Somali kitten, being held for cleaning.

are abdominal distension (potbelly), and increased water intake with concurrent increased urination. It is usually seen in older cats and it is especially prevalent in cats that have received steroid (cortisone) therapy.

Diabetes mellitus is another disease of older cats and has symptoms similar to those discussed immediately above. Diabetic cats are often treated with insulin injections that can be given by owners. Dietary control is another important aspect of therapy.

All of the above hormonal diseases are very complex and are diagnosed only by physical examinations and laboratory tests.

Toxicosis (Poisoning)

Cats' grooming habits often get them in trouble with poisons. They lick their feet clean, no matter what they may have stepped in. Therefore, outdoor cats are more likely to be poisoned than indoor pets. If they walk across a lawn that has been sprayed with a bug poison, they are sure to pick up some of the insecticide on their feet, and, thus, they may be poisoned when they lick it off. Most of the outdoor insecticides are highly toxic to cats and if you suspect your cat has been exposed to one, you should call for professional help immediately.

- One of the most common causes of outside pet poisoning is ethylene glycol (antifreeze). It is doubly dangerous because it has a rather sweet taste that some cats find quite palatable. If your automobile leaks antifreeze on the garage floor, or if you add antifreeze to your car's radiator, be very sure all spills are cleaned up immediately. Ethylene glycol, when ingested, causes kidney destruction, and is usually fatal in both cats and dogs. There is no specific detoxifying treatment available, and dialysis and supportive therapy are usually ineffective.
- Boric acid is a common household insecticide used for roach and ant control. It is generally thought to be safe around animals, and is only mildly toxic to cats, causing diarrhea and excessive salivation.
- Rotenone, a natural plant-origin insecticide, is also generally considered nontoxic, but if ingested by a cat, it may cause lethargy.
- Cleaning and disinfecting agents can easily be the cause of toxicosis if not kept out of the reach of your cats.

- Certain houseplants contain toxins that may poison cats. If your pet munches on your plants, consult your veterinarian about the possible dangers from the specific vegetation that it enjoys. Plant-eating cats can usually be trained to stay away from houseplants by growing some wheat or oats in a window box. Most cats like to browse on those grasses, and when available, they will defer their attention to them instead of eating your philodendra.
- Human drugs such as aspirin, ibuprofens, acetaminophens, antihistamines, and some antibiotics can be dangerous when ingested by cats. Keep all drugs, household chemicals, and cleaning agents locked safely away from the curious felines of the household.

The propensity of cats to lick their feet predisposes them to poisoning.

When to Retire a Breeding Queen

As discussed previously, shortly after a litter is weaned, the queen will begin another estrus period and start the whole reproductive process over again. As you have no doubt perceived, cats are well equipped for extensive reproductive lives. Although several situations require a queen to be spayed to preserve her health or save her life, most well-managed queens don't suffer those threatening conditions. They continue to produce kittens as long as their owners supply toms at the appropriate times.

If you are just launching your career in cat breeding, you may not be terribly interested in terminating the reproductive life of your young, beautiful queens. Those animals were purchased, cared for, and shown specifically to raise kittens. Of course, most cat breeders are quite attached to their breeding stock. Often the queens are friends and companions first, and their ability to reproduce is secondary. In any case, part of good cat breeding management is recognition of the appropriate time to retire a breeding queen.

After five or six years of kitten production, most queens begin to deliver and raise smaller litters. Sometimes the kittens are not as strong and vital as those of earlier litters. Failure to conceive may require repeated breedings. With fewer kittens per litter, sometimes the kittens are larger and dystocias may be faced more frequently. Those situations are often accompanied by general condition loss in the queen. She becomes less robust and thinner, and her coat isn't as glossy as when she was young.

These are indications that it is time to look to the future of the queen. When a queen is to be retired, whatever the reason, have her spayed! That surgery will not only stop estrous cycles, it will reduce the probability of mammary tumors, and prevent metritis, pyometra, ovarian tumors, and other intact queen problems.

Spaying is one of the least understood procedures among cat breeders. Abdominal surgery that is done under general anesthetic is not without risk, but in the hands of experienced surgeons, the risks are very minimal. Young, healthy cats present the lowest risk, but even pregnant or older females rarely suffer serious difficulties with the surgery.

Older breeding queens' general health and appearance are often improved by spaying. Contrary to popular myths, cats don't get fat when they are spayed. They become obese because they consume greater amounts of calories than they burn. Dietary control will prevent obesity, but spaying won't cause it!

Male breeding animals usually enjoy longer reproductive lives than females, and if kept confined, there are no particular reasons to castrate breeding toms except to change the odor of their urine, and perhaps to curtail their spraying habits. After tomcat habits are established and practiced for many years, attitudes and personalities will probably not be greatly improved by castration. If toms have been continually handled during their breeding lives, and except for their urine spraying, they are good pets, castration will certainly help improve their pet status.

Feline Geriatric Disorders

Senile cataracts are caused by aging of the lens of the eyes. The normally soft, gelatinous lens material becomes hardened and opaque and appears as a white or blue structure behind the iris. Cataracts rarely cause total blindness, and an old cat's senses of smell, touch, and hearing usually remain sharp enough to compensate for the loss of visual acuity.

Osteoarthritis is an old cat condition that causes joint swelling and loss of normal limb functions. Arthritic pain can sometimes be reduced with medication, but you should not attempt home therapy without professional advice. Aspirin and several other human anti-inflammatory drugs are toxic to cats unless the dosage is meticulously calculated.

Deafness is observed in a few very old cats. It is usually a degenerative condition for which there is rarely any treatment. Fortunately, old cats seem oblivious to their loss of hearing. Owners and deaf house pets manage to communicate through touch.

Kidney failure is a degenerative disease that claims many lives. Aged animals compensate for a gradual loss of kidney function by drinking increasing amounts of water. When they are unable to consume and eliminate sufficient quantities of water, they may become uremic. If kidney compromise is discovered early, special diets are available to reduce the stress on those organs. When your old cat's thirst increases, and it is observed making frequent trips to the litter box, consult your veterinarian.

Giving your cat a pill is easy, if you take time to do it right.

Giving Your Cat a Pill

Fortunately, many feline drugs are now packaged in flavored, liquid formulations and dropper bottles that make medicine administration relatively simple. Sometimes, it is necessary to give your kitten a pill. For many years, I used a technique that rarely failed. The entire procedure should only take about 10 to 15 seconds from the time you get the patient wrapped up and sitting on a counter.

First, put a small amount of butter or margarine in a saucer, near the pill, on a countertop. Wrap your cat in a large towel, with only its head protruding from the towel cocoon. Place your left hand (assuming that you are right-handed), palm down on top of the cat's head. Then grip its head with the tip of your thumb on the right cheek, and your index or middle finger on the left. Press the tips of your finger and thumb inward, forcing the cat's upper lips between its upper

and lower rear molar teeth. As you squeeze the lips inward, tip the cat's head back, so that its nose points toward the ceiling, over its back.

When that position is reached, the lower jaw will open. Drop the pill over the top of the tongue, directly into the throat. Immediately relax your grip on your patient's head, and as you do so, dip your right index finger in the butter and wipe it on the nostrils of the patient. The cat will quickly lick its nose to clear the nostrils. In doing so, its tongue comes forward, the cat swallows, and the pill is on its way to the stomach (see illustration above).

Symptoms of Illnesses

Cat owners are alerted to their pets' illnesses by changes in attitudes, appetites, and habits, but sometimes it is difficult to find meaningful criteria and terms to convey these observations to their veterinarians. In addition to terminology, think carefully about the duration of the symptoms that you have observed. They may be associated with some particular event in the pet's life. For instance, did the symptoms begin a few days after the cat was boarded, a change in diet was made, or a houseplant was consumed? Make notes of your observations and use them when you call your veterinarian for advice.

- Temperature elevation is a very meaningful sign that is easily obtained. Anytime you suspect illness in your pet, take its temperature. The normal rectal temperature of a cat is between 101 and 102°F (38.3 –39°C).

- Locomotion problems might be described as difficulty in rising, lameness in one leg, falling when attempting to walk, or staggering.

- If there is a visible swelling, pinpoint the location and make a size comparison to a known object: the size of a match head, a marble, or a golf ball. Check to see if the swelling has a scab, and if it is tender to your touch.

- When your pet loses its appetite, check to see if it will eat one type of food, but not another. If it refuses food, does it eat a mouthful, then stop; or does it show no interest in any food? If it picks up its food, then drops it, that is also important.

- If your cat seems to have urination difficulty, note the specific symptoms, such as straining and crying. Check to see if any urine is being passed, and look for urine in strange places. Check the odor and color of urine if any is found. Watch the cat's drinking habits to see if it is drinking more or less than normal, or none at all. Does vomiting follow its eating or drinking?

- When a digestive disorder is suspected, check the litter box for the consistency, color, and odor of the feces. Is it hard, dry, and white colored, or liquid, black, and foul smelling? Does the cat defecate in strange places? Is there foreign material in the feces such as crayons, hair mats, or foil?

- When vomiting is the primary symptom, check the vomitus for food, foreign material, worms, blood, mucus, or hair mats. Watch to see if the vomiting occurs frequently, or only on rare occasions. Does the vomiting follow coughing episodes?

- Respiratory difficulty may be further described by noting whether the cat's breathing is relaxed and smooth, or labored and deep. Raspy sounds or panting are often signs of serious respiratory problems. Is the primary symptom sneezing, and if so, how often does it occur?

- Always check the cat's mucous membrane color, to see if its gums are pale, white, dark red, blue-tinged, or a normal pink.

- If concerned about a skin abnormality, make notes relative to the location of hairless patches, inflamed, red lesions, or raised, puffy spots. Note whether the hair is brittle and dry, and if there is a general thinning of the coat. Are there any scabs present, or oozing, bloody, or moist lesions?
- Another important feature of any illness is the cat's attitude. Observe whether it is particularly grouchy and irritable and wishes to be left alone, or if it is quite affectionate. Does it hide from the family? Watch the pet's body posture; notice whether it lies down and sits normally, or prefers to stand.
- A cat's eye appearance will often help qualify certain diseases. Check to see if the pupils are dilated, constricted to pinpoint size, or normal. Is the third eyelid pulled up and very apparent in the corner of the eye? Are the eyes dull and not responsive to changes of scenes? Note the quantity and color of any ocular discharge seen. Is the cat squinting through red and inflamed eyes?
- Changes in the pet's weight may be important. Has it recently lost or gained weight?

Become more aware of signs to look for when you think your feline friends are not up to snuff, but don't attempt to diagnose and treat your cat's illnesses based on the information provided. The preceding pages are intended to improve your communication with your veterinarian and improve your knowledge of some of the more common cat diseases and their symptoms.

Euthanasia

It is normal for pet owners to refuse to entertain thoughts of the inevitable loss of their pets. Your feline companion will live for many years, but eventually the end will come. Hopefully it will be quick and painless for both pet and owner. In certain prolonged disease conditions such as inoperable cancer that do not respond to therapy, you may consider euthanasia. Life and death decisions must be made by owners with the guidance of animal health care professionals. Euthanasia of a pet, in the hands of an experienced professional, can be a quiet, painless and comfortable way to end a pet's life.

Chapter 15

Registration of Purebred Cats

Each of the several feline registry organizations has its own registration rules, but they are somewhat similar. For your convenience, the names of cat registries are included in Useful Literature and Addresses, page 157. A few general ideas are offered here to guide you.

Presuming that your queen is a registered purebred, you should begin the litter registration process as soon as the kittens are born. From the information given to you when you acquired your queen, you can find the address and phone number of her registry. Write or telephone that organization, requesting a litter registration application. Once it is received, simply follow the directions that accompany it. The completed application should be returned to the registry, together with a nominal fee, and you will shortly receive individual registration papers for each of your kittens. Check the kitten registration documents over carefully to be sure that the correct sex, color, and markings are listed.

Pedigrees can be obtained from the registries, or you can purchase blank pedigrees from a pet supply store and fill them in yourself, using the pedigrees of your queen and the sire.

Cat shows are held and judged according to rules of the individual associations. Information and show rules can be obtained from the cat registries. Shows are well advertised in cat magazines that are obtained in pet supply stores and at newsstands.

References

Beaver, Bonnie V. 1977. Mating Behavior in the Cat. *Veterinary Clinics of North America,* 7, no. 4: 729–33.

Birchard and Sherding. 1994. *Saunders Manual of Small Animal Practice.* Philadelphia: W. B. Saunders Company.

Burke, Thomas J. 1977. Fertility Control in the Cat. *Veterinary Clinics of North America,* 7, no. 4: 699–703.

Gilroy, Beverly A. et.al. 1986. Cesarean Section. *Veterinary Clinics of North America,* 16, no. 3: 483–93.

Herron, Mary A. 1977. Feline Reproduction. *Veterinary Clinics of North America.* 7, no. 4: 715–21.

Holzworth. 1987. *Diseases of The Cat.* Philadelphia: W.B. Saunders Company.

Hudson and Hamilton. 1993. *Atlas of Feline Anatomy for Veterinarians.* Philadelphia: W.B. Saunders Company

Johnston, Shirley. 1987. Clinical Manifestations of Fetal Loss in the Dog and Cat. *Veterinary Clinics of North America.* 17, no. 3: 535–51.

Kirk. 1995. *Current Veterinary Therapy XII,* Philadelphia: W.B. Saunders Company.

Lawler, Dennis F. et.al. 1986. Nutrition and Management of Reproduction in the Cat. *Veterinary Clinics of North America.* 16, no. 3: 495–517.

McCurnin and Paffenbarger. 1991. *Small Animal Physical Diagnosis and Clinical Procedures.* Philadelphia: W. B. Saunders Company.

Monson, William J. 1987. Orphan Rearing of Puppies and Kittens. *Veterinary Clinics of North America.* 17, no. 3: 567–76.

Nelson, Richard W., et.al. 1986. Pyometra, *Veterinary Clinics of North America.* 16, no. 3: 561–75.

Papich et.al. 1986. Drug Therapy During Pregnancy and in the Neonate. *Veterinary Clinics of North America.* 16, no. 3: 525–37.

Roth, James A. 1987. Possible Association of Thymus Dysfunction with Fading Syndromes in Puppies and Kittens. *Veterinary Clinics of North America.* 17, no. 3: 603–15.

Schmidt, Patricia M. 1986. Feline Breeding Management. *Veterinary Clinics of North America.* 16, no. 3: 435–49.

Stubbs, W. Preston. 1993. Early Neutering in the Dog and Cat. *Proceedings of Canine Theriogenology Short Course.*

Glossary

Active immunity: Long-lasting immunity; one produced by the animal in response to antigens.

Ailurophile: One who loves cats.

Ailurophobe: One who hates or fears cats.

Ambient temperature: Surrounding environmental temperature.

Amniotic: The thin membrane forming a closed sac around an embryo.

Anamnesis: Memory or recall.

Anemia: Reduced hemoglobin or quantity of red blood cells.

Anestrus: The fourth, inactive stage of the female estrous cycle.

Anorexia: Lack of appetite.

Antibiotic: Product used to kill or interrupt reproduction of bacteria.

Antibodies: Proteins that, when stimulated by an antigen, act against that specific antigen. Important element of immune response.

Antigenicity: The ability or propensity to stimulate immune response within an animal.

Ataxia: Inability to move about voluntarily.

Atresia: Absence of normal opening.

Biologic: A biological product, such as a vaccine, used in medicine.

Biological: Relating to life or the living process.

Castration: The surgical removal of both of a male's testicles.

Catabolism: The breakdown of organic materials, releasing energy.

Cervix: The constricted opening of the female's uterus into the vagina.

Cesarean: The surgical delivery of offspring through an abdominal incision.

Clavicle: The collarbone.

Colostrum: The milk secreted for a few days following parturition, containing high levels of protein and antibodies.

Congenital: Condition present at birth.

Corpus luteum: The small, white scar, formerly ovarian follicle, from which an ovum has been released.

Cryosurgery: Destruction of tissues by freezing; usually uses liquid nitrogen as freezing agent.

Cryptorchid: Both testicles retained in the male's abdomen or inguinal canal.

Dehydration: Unnatural body fluid deficit.

Diagnosis: Specific cause of a disease.

Diestrus: The third stage of the canine estrous cycle that includes pregnancy. Formerly called metestrus.

Dysplasia: An abnormality of development, often referring to joints, but may be applied to soft tissue structures.

Dystocia: Difficult or prolonged labor.

Ectoparasites: Parasites, such as fleas or ticks, that live on the host's skin.

Electrolyte solution: An aqueous solution containing various essential mineral ions.

ELISA (enzyme-linked immunosorbent assay): A blood analysis test technique used to determine serum hormone or antibody levels.

Embryo: The early developmental stage of an unborn animal.

Endemic: Occurring in, or native to, a particular region or area.

Endometrium: The highly vascular lining of the uterus.

Estrogen: Female sex hormone.

Estrous cycle: The endocrine and generative changes taking place in a female from the beginning of one estrus period to the beginning of the next.

Estrus: Feline heat period during which a female will accept a male, ovulate, and conceive.

Euthanasia: The professional, painless act of ending an animal's life for humane reasons.

Evisceration: Portions of intestine protruding from an abdominal wound.

Fallopian tube: Another name for oviduct, leading from the ovary to the tip of each uterine horn.

Feces: Bowel excretions.

Feral: Undomesticated or wild.

Fetus: The second stage of an unborn kitten, usually used after about two or three weeks of gestation.

Felidae: The taxonomic family in which felines are listed.

Follicle: The small ovarian depression in which ova (eggs) develop.

FSH (follicle stimulating hormone): A hormone that originates in the pituitary gland and has its primary effect on the ovaries.

Gamete: Male or female germ cell; sperm or ovum.

Genitalia: The reproductive organs of males or females.

Gravid: Containing one or more fetuses; pregnant.

Hematocrit: The percentage of packed red blood; cells in the whole blood, used to determine anemia and dehydration.

Hemobartonella: A blood parasite of cats causing anemia.

Hemorrhage: Loss of blood.

Hereditary: Genetically transmissible condition.

Hernia: Protrusion of an organ or tissue through an unnatural opening in the body.

Hormone: A secretory product originating from certain body cells, inciting a specific effect on other cells.

Hypothermia: Having a body temperature below normal.

Inbreeding: Breeding closely related animals, such as father to daughter, sister to brother, or son to mother.

Intact: Either a male or female cat that hasn't been neutered.

Interestrous period: The interval between estrous periods.

Intramuscular: Injected into the muscle.

Intranasal: Administered into the nostrils by spray.

Intravenous: Injected into blood veins.

Intromission: The insertion of a tom's penis into the queen's vagina during copulation.

K/cal or kilocalorie: Also known as large calorie; is the amount of heat energy required to raise 1 kilogram of water from 15 to 16°C. Equivalent to 3.968 British thermal units.

Lactation: Normal milk production.

Laparoscope: A fiber-optic instrument that is introduced into the abdomen through a very small incision.

Laparoscopy: A visual examination conducted by means of a laparoscope.

LH (lutenizing hormone): A hormone originating from the pituitary gland, acting primarily on the ovarian follicles of a queen.

Linebreeding: Breeding related animals within a bloodline, usually cousins, uncles.

Malignant: Uncontrolled growth, usually relating to tumors.

Mastectomy: The surgical removal of a queen's mammary gland.

Meconium: Dark, greenish feces that accumulates in the bowel of fetuses and passes from the bowel shortly after birth.

Metabolism: The sum process of buildup and breakdown of organic matter within an organism.

Metritis: Uterine inflammation.

Microorganisms: Organisms of microscopic or submicroscopic size, such as bacteria and viruses.

Monestrous: Experiencing one estrus period each season.

Monorchid: One testicle retained in the abdomen; the other is descended normally into the scrotum.

Moribund: Being in the state of dying or approaching death.

Mucous membranes: The tissue rich in mucus glands that lines body passages that communicate with the exterior, such as the mouth, nasal cavity, and conjunctiva.

Multiparous: Having experienced previous parturition.

Nematode: Any of several intestinal roundworms.

Neonatal: Newborn or infant kitten.

Obese: Containing excessive quantities of body fat.

Ophthalmic: Pertaining to the eyes.

Organism: A living being.

Ovariohysterectomy: Surgical removal of the queen's ovaries and uterus.

Ovary: The female's paired abdominal organs that produce ova (eggs) and reproductive hormones.

Oviduct: The tubes leading from the ovaries to the uterine horns (Fallopian tubes).

Ovulation: The process whereby ova are released from the ovarian follicles into the oviducts.

Ovum: Egg, or the female haploid reproductive cell (plural is *ova).*

Palpation: To examine by touch.

Papillae: Spiny protuberances on the surface of a cat's tongue and a male cat's penis.

Parturition: The process of giving birth to offspring.

Passive immunity: Temporary protection from a specific disease, conferred by obtaining antibodies from another source.

Pathogen: An organism capable of causing a disease.

Perineum: The body area extending from the anus downward, including external genital openings.

Pheromone: A chemical produced by animals that stimulates a behavioral response by another of the same species.

Pituitary gland (hypophysis): Small gland located at the base of the brain, producing many different hormones.

Placenta: The saclike organ that envelops a fetus and attaches to the lining of the dam's uterus, providing nutrition to unborn kittens.

Polydactyly: Possessing extra toes.

Post parturient: Occurring shortly after queening.

Proestrus: The first stage of a queen's estrous cycle manifested by behavioral abnormalities.

Progesterone: A female sex hormone originating first from the corpus luteum, and later from the placenta.

Prolapse: The slipping of a body organ from its normal position.

Prostate: One of several secondary sex glands.

Pruritus: Itch.

Pseudocyesis: Outward signs of pregnancy without kitten production (false pregnancy).

Puberty: The age at which an animal becomes capable of sexually reproducing.

Purebred: The progeny of parents of the same registered breed.

Purulent: Containing pus.

Queen: Female cat.

Queening: Giving birth to kittens.

Resorption: Breaking down and assimilating embryos or fetuses without outward, visible signs of illness.

RIA (radioimmunoassay): A blood analysis test technique used to determine serum hormone levels.

Ringer's solution: An electrolytic solution containing sodium chloride, potassium chloride, and calcium chloride in specific concentrations.

Semen: The composite ejaculate of a male, containing sperm and glandular fluids.

Spay: Surgical removal of a queen's ovaries and uterus (ovariohysterectomy).

Sperm: The mobile male reproductive cells (or gametes) that originate in the testicle.

Subcutaneous: Beneath the skin, such as a subcutaneous injection.

Taxonomy or taxonomic: The orderly classification and naming of animals according to natural relationships.

Tom: A male cat, usually reserved for intact males.

Toxemia: An abnormal, diseased state caused by toxins or poisons in the blood.

Toxic: Suffering from a poison or toxin that may be chemical, bacterial, or metabolic in origin.

Ultrasound: Diagnostic image production by sound waves passed through the body.

Urethra: Urine transporting tube leading from the bladder to the exterior of the animal.

Uterus: The queen's hollow reproductive organ consisting of a body and two horns in which embryos are attached.

Vaccine: Man-made antigenic product designed to elicit an immune response when introduced into the body.

Vagina: The hollow female reproductive organ situated between the vulva and the cervix (vaginal vault).

Vector: An organism or object that transmits a disease.

Virulent: Having the capacity to produce disease.

Vulva: The outermost female reproductive structure composed of two vertical lips.

X ray: Diagnostic image production by radiation passed through the body.

Zygote: The cell formed by the union of two gametes (sperm and ovum); the recognizable beginning of an embryo.

Useful Literature and Addresses

Books

Behrend, K. and Wegler, M. *The Complete Book of Cat Care: How to Raise a Happy and Healthy Cat.* Barron's Educational Series, Inc., Hauppauge, New York, 1991.

Carlson, Delbert G., D.V.M., and Giffin, James M., M.D. *Cat Owner's Veterinary Handbook,* New York: Howell Book House, 1983.

Daly, Carol Himsel, D.V.M. *Caring for Your Sick Cat.* Barron's Educational Series, Inc., Hauppauge, New York, 1994.

Fogle, Bruce. *The Cat's Mind: Understanding Your Cat's Behavior.* New York: Howell Book House, 1992.

Frye, Fredric. *First Aid for Your Cat.* Barron's Educational Series, Inc., Hauppauge, New York, 1987.

Maggitti, Phil. *Before You Buy That Kitten.* Barron's Educational Series, Inc., Hauppauge, New York, 1995.

Tabor, Roger. *The Wild Life of the Domestic Cat.* London: Arrow Books Limited, 1983.

Turner, Dennis C. and Bateson, Patrick, eds. *The Domestic Cat: the Biology of its Behavior.* Cambridge, England: Cambridge Univeristy Press, 1988.

Wright, Michael and Walter, Sally, ed. *The Book of the Cat.* New York, Summit Books, 1980.

Cat Registries

American Cat Association
8101 Katherine Avenue
Panorama City, CA 91402
818-782-6080

American Cat Fanciers
Association
P.O. Box 203
Point Lookout, MO 65726
417-334-5430

Canadian Cat Association
83 Kennedy Road South
Unit 1805
Brampton, Ontario
Canada L6W 3P3
905-459-1481

Cat Fanciers' Association
P.O. Box 1005
Manasquan, NJ 08738-1005
908-528-9797

Cat Fanciers' Federation
9509 Montgomery Road
Cincinnati, OH 45242
513-984-1841

The International Cat
Association
P.O. Box 2684
Harlingen, TX 78551
210-428-8046

Cat Magazines
Cats
2750-A South Ridgewood Avenue
South Daytona, FL 32110

Cat Fancy
P.O. Box 6050
Mission Viejo, CA 92690

Cats U.S.A.
P.O. Box 55811
Boulder, CO 80322-5811
303-786-7652

I Love Cats
Grass Roots Publishing Co.
950 Third Avenue
New York, NY 10022

Cat World International
P.O. Box 35635
Phoenix, AZ 85069-5635
602-995-1822

Index